Tim Fischer's
Outback Heroes

Dear Shirley & Rich

Happy Christmas
2002

Bishy

Tim Fischer's
Outback Heroes

AND COMMUNITIES
THAT COUNT

Peter Rees and Tim Fischer

ALLEN&UNWIN

First published in 2002

Allen & Unwin
83 Alexander Street
Crows Nest NSW 2065
Australia
Phone: (61 2) 8425 0100
Fax: (61 2) 9906 2218
Email: info@allenandunwin.com
Web: www.allenandunwin.com

National Library of Australia
Cataloguing-in-Publication entry:

Rees, Peter, 1948- .
    Tim Fischer's outback heroes and communities that count.

    Includes index.
    ISBN 1 86508 831 5.

    1. Australians. 2. Country life - Australia I. Fischer,
    Tim, 1946- . II. Title.

994

Set in 12/16.4 pt Bembo by Bookhouse, Sydney
Printed by Griffin Press, Adelaide

10 9 8 7 6 5 4 3 2 1

This book is dedicated to all the leaders and communities across Australia who have contributed to the new spirit of the bush. We salute all of you.

Foreword

2002 has been designated the Year of the Outback.

The Outback

The Inland

The Country

The Bush

are all used to describe that great area of Australia where most of us choose *not* to live. Most Australians cling to the south-west and south-east coasts like fly spots on the edge of a picture frame—'looking off the southern edge', as David Buchanan described it, for meaning and cultural sustenance—measuring our worth by constantly proclaiming the sophistication of our (world class) cities.

But the romance is out there; the Australia tourists visualise and want to see is out there; the myths are out there. And there are people out there doing well.

School holidays when I was a child were spent on the farms of friends or relatives assisting with shearing, seeding and harvesting. My first earned cash was 9 shillings for a week rousabouting for a couple of shearers whose offsider hadn't turned up. They also allowed me to accompany them to the local agricultural show, which must have been pretty embarrassing for these two as I was 9 years old with a long ponytail!

How country towns have changed since then. There are fewer people for a start—larger farms mean fewer country friends/cousins for city kids to holiday with. In contrast, over the past decade there has been a movement of indigenous people back to traditional lands. As well, many towns are tidy—civic pride is obvious and everywhere. Each one has a craft shop or an art gallery.

Perhaps Tim and Peter's next book could be about the interest in the arts in rural Australia. Several country centres in Western Australia boast far better theatre facilities than Perth can provide. Large companies such as Woodside, Hammersley and BHP are making great contributions to rural communities, supporting visits from orchestras and theatre, ballet and opera companies. In Western Australia, the Balidu Contemporary Art Society, the Esperance Gallery, the Kelleberrin Centre and Williams Coachhouse Gallery, are all dynamic organisations. The town of Waroona welcomes travellers with twelve remarkable sculptures that tell the town's story. And did you know that every two years Grafton hosts a Philosophy, Science and Theology Festival?

But is this how city folk perceive the Outback now? Not at all!

It is long overdue for a book to be published that highlights positive and motivated people and communities beyond Australia's big capital cities, to help provide a balance against negative perceptions of the bush. Over recent years stories of failure and hardship have dominated the media. Perhaps it has always been thus, and perhaps this is necessary because for many people and communities there is untold misery and suffering and decline.

However, it would be wrong to allow pessimism to completely dominate and obliterate the positive, especially as this compounds the lack of confidence, which then undermines vital new ideas and investment in rural and regional Australia.

The authors, Peter Rees and Tim Fischer, both know coastal and country Australia well. They also know how to recognise the positive and highlight this in a compelling way. Peter comes from a media background (based in Wagga in the early days and then Canberra), while Tim is the Boy from Boree Creek—the farmer and former army officer who was the Acting Prime Minister of Australia on sixteen occasions.

One of the intriguing dimensions of many of the extraordinary selection of stories in *Tim Fischer's Outback Heroes* is how many people had spectacular failures en route to ultimate success. They got up off the floor and tried again, with new purpose and new ideas. They were not scared off by their mistakes, but learnt from them. And they didn't rely on 'Aorta', as in 'Aorta do something about it' or 'Aorta help me . . . '. They did it on their own without relying on government assistance.

This book points to the fact that renewal and recovery is an ongoing dynamic process with many facets. I thoroughly recommend it to city folk who need to understand how things have changed 'out back' and to country folk who need inspiration and confirmation.

Janet Holmes a Court

Contents

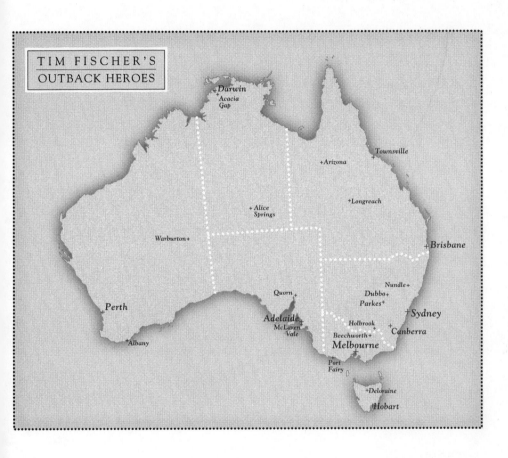

TIM FISCHER'S
OUTBACK HEROES

+Darwin
Acacia
Gap

Townsville

+Arizona

+Longreach

+Alice
Springs

Warburton+

+Brisbane

Nundle+
Dubbo+
Parkes+

Quorn+
Sydney
Adelaide+
Perth
McLaren Canberra
Vale
Holbrook
+Albany Beechworth+
Melbourne
Port
Fairy

+Deloraine
+Hobart

Outback
Stars

The Outback. The word has mythic status and stirs deep emotions in any Australian. For 200 years the Outback has been an integral part of Australian folklore. Out there beyond the comfort of the cities, in the vast emptiness of the inland, it has shaped people's thinking. Whether scrub or plains, it conjures images that are steeped in legend and tradition. But where is it?

Generally, it is regarded as the regions remote from settled districts, but confusion abounds as no-one can be too sure where the Outback begins and where it ends. Writer Bill Wannan has noted that Bourke, in far north-western New South Wales, was considered by people living along Australia's eastern seaboard in colonial times to be one of civilisation's last outposts. 'Hence,' he wrote in his *Australian Folklore* dictionary published in 1970, 'the country to the westward of Bourke was "the farthest far outback"'. Wannan earned a reputation as an authority on legends and popular allusions and has quoted a bushman's description in *Bill Wannan's Tales from Back o' Bourke* to loosely back this up: 'Outback is away out west, out in the never-never, where the crows fly backwards to keep the dust out of their eyes; it's away out west o'sunset and right out back o'beyond; it's the great open spaces where men are men and dogs are miracles; it's away out—well, it's away out back. Yer can't miss it.'

In his verse, 'Outback', Henry Lawson portrayed it as harsh, unforgiving country peopled by itinerants and travellers:

> For time means tucker, and tramp you must where the scrubs
>   and plains are wide,
> With seldom a track that a man can trust, or a mountain peak
>   to guide;
> All day long in the dust and heat—when summer is on the
>   track—
> With stinted stomachs and blistered feet, they carry their swags
>   Out Back.

Lawson did not see the Outback through rose-tinted glasses. He chided poets who 'invariably' got the coast scenery mixed up with that of the Outback: 'We wish to Heaven that Australian writers would leave off trying to make a paradise out of the Out Back Hell.' Craig McGregor in his 1960s book, *Profile of Australia*, agreed about the toughness of the challenge when he observed: 'In the outback Australians have had to wrestle with some of the harshest physical conditions in the world.'

In 1978, the former United States presidential contender, Senator Eugene McCarthy, in a visit to Australia was intrigued by the term. He observed that in the US, if one lived in the interior it was common to refer to the east as 'out east', and to the west as 'out west'. 'This is not so in Australia,' McCarthy said.

'Whether an Australian is from the north, south, east or west, the interior is out!' At the start of the Year of the Outback in 2002, founder and chairman of the event, Bruce Campbell, told the *Sydney Morning Herald* that the Outback could not be defined. 'It's symbolic of the whole country. We have all got some of it in us,' he contended. In the context of this book the term includes everywhere beyond the boundaries of the capital cities—and with due respect to Henry Lawson, some rural coastal communities have also been included.

Despite the bush's place in the nation's folklore, for many city people these days, what lies outside urban boundaries is often an unknown landscape, destined not to be part of their life experience, beyond cinema screens or romantic bush ballads. In recent years a divide has arisen between the cities and the bush, with a perception that somehow there's a different country out there, Outback. Indeed, Sydney and Melbourne have become virtual city-states within states, such is their size and economic strength.

However, a nation has many components and grows from the deeds of many people. The most fundamental components are communities, and Australia needs prosperous rural and regional communities as much as it needs prosperous city communities. Seven million people live outside the capital cities, and regional Australia, which has a third of the workforce, accounts for half of the nation's export income. They provide an admirable backbone.

If heroes are people who do things out of the ordinary then the Australian Outback is rich with them. They are the women and men who are making their mark at a time of great change in Australia. They are people who have been—and still are— prepared to take a risk, who create an opportunity by thinking laterally and flouting conventional wisdom. They are entrepreneurs, positive people who are often less constrained by society's expectations. This is the credo of the modern bush.

But they also have a wider vision. Invariably they are people who have a strong sense of community and understand the importance of giving something back. An unshakeable faith in not just their region but Australia as a nation flows from this. Another common value is a tendency to a more holistic view of the rural landscape; the importance of a balance between agriculture and the environment; between farms and towns; that they need each other if they are both to survive.

The people who succeed in achieving their dreams in the Outback today are people with such values. Many of them have done it tough, flirting with failure but pushing through successfully. So many of these stories of achievement evolve from strong personal relationships; often couples who balance and optimise each other's qualities, enabling goals and dreams to be realised.

These are people like Roger Fletcher, the drover who with his wife, Gail, founded a sheepmeat empire in Dubbo; Tom and Christine O'Toole, who run an incredibly successful bakery in Beechworth; Steve and Karen Birkbeck, who established a flourishing international sandalwood oil business; Peter and Judy Howarth, who bought virtually a whole town that was dying and revitalised it; Richard and Judi Makim, who have overturned generations of conventional grazing practices on their station in far north Queensland; and Mick and Shauna Denigan, who saw the opportunity from the Northern Territory to use the internet to establish an international market for whips. Then there is Jane Bennett, who with the help of her family has pushed the boundaries to become one of Australia's first female cheesemakers.

Communities, however, are crucial in these stories. Communities are not just good transport services or attractive locations; they are people. There are towns on picturesque inland rivers and coastal villages adjoining unspoiled beaches that are caught in a spiral of decline. Indeed, some towns are dying—drive up and down the main streets and see the 'For Sale' signs. No-one wants to buy.

Other towns, such as Narrandera in southern New South Wales and Northam, an hour east of Perth, have not fully realised their potential over recent decades. In the case of Narrandera it has many strong features including its position next to the Murrumbidgee River, being at the junction of the Sturt and Newell highways, a particularly beautiful town vista, a good airport and an operational rail link. Decisions by previous New South Wales governments in the 1950s saw Leeton develop as the service centre for the growing Murrumbidgee Irrigation Area ahead of Narrandera. But even this should not have prevented Narrandera realising its full potential.

A combination of divisive factors, including too often a less than united Narrandera Shire Council, led to the town slipping further behind Wagga Wagga, an hour's drive to the east, and Griffith, an hour's drive to the west. Real attempts are now being made to rectify this and to highlight some of the town's outstanding features, including one of the state's best inland swimming and water skiing recreational complexes at Lake Talbot.

For years Northam lacked a four- or five-star motel, notwithstanding its location on the highway between Perth to Kalgoorlie and across the Nullarbor to the east. The nearby

town of York developed its tourism approach more compre-
hensively and more quickly than Northam and in a way that
saw Northam drift along for too long. In recent years Northam's
renewed efforts to revamp local accommodation and promote
the commuter train to and from Perth have made a difference.

While many would regard it as a harsh judgment, both
Narrandera and Northam could have doubled their 1960 population if their full potential had been realised over the intervening
period. In some respects they have been shown up by the efforts
of smaller towns such as the verandah town of Lockhart and the
old railway junction town of Junee, both in southern New
South Wales, or the busy Western Australian town of Busselton,
and Kalgoorlie successfully combining tourism and mining. In
the case of Narrandera and Northam, governments as well as
local factors are to blame, but the good news is that both these
towns have now turned the corner and show some signs of
renewed activity and development.

At Narrandera, the Lake Talbot swimming complex has been
revamped, and the New South Wales Fisheries Visitors Centre
excels but the promotion of both needs more vigour. At
Northam, the riverside walk and park has been beautified, along
with a memorial to Victoria Cross winner, Jim Throssell, who
at the big welcome home in his honour announced to the
crowd his support for communism.

When a business closes in a country town it often has a
knock-on effect that is far more noticeable than in a city
community. Because the service or product is no longer available, people and businesses look elsewhere. Inevitably, some will
leave, re-igniting the gloomy downward spiral that generates
media headlines. Certainly, in some towns there is a listlessness

and diminished resolve after a series of blows that have eaten away at the fabric holding the community together.

Such decline is not universal. In other towns there is a busyness and a perceptible air of confidence that goes hand-in-hand with expanding economic opportunities. This underlines the resilience of the Outback, where people's horizons are not hemmed in by urban limits and where there's a willingness to 'have a go'. There is a determination to find new products for new markets; to find new ways of doing old things. Integral to this is a willingness to question old practices and re-invent them to do things better.

There are communities without obvious attractions or resources enjoying revival and renewal. The difference is often dynamic local leadership. This may occur through chambers of commerce, councils, main street committees or service clubs. It can often be the energy of an individual who, in working towards a goal, creates a momentum that brings the community along. The result is a motivated community where cohesion and pride are clearly evident.

Successful communities are groups of people who can recognise and accept difference and still work together. Towns like Deloraine in northern Tasmania have faced up to such challenges and harvested not just greater cohesion but new growth opportunities. In Western Australia, the Indigenous community of Warburton took stock of its situation. It identified long-term goals, in the process building the largest community-owned collection of Indigenous art in Australia. As well, Warburton artists are making remarkable glass art displayed in an award-winning cultural centre.

Communities create different ways to survive. Some find answers within their community; still others benefit from outside

Tim Fischer admiring Taparta Bates' Ngaanyatjarra glass art during a visit to Warburton. (Courtesy of Newspix)

involvement by creating attractions to encourage visitors. Port Fairy in Victoria, for instance, has established itself as a festival town. Likewise the New South Wales town of Parkes does festivals. But that is not the only reason for the confidence one finds on Parkes' streets, for the town is an emerging national transport hub, thanks to the foresight of one man in particular, Bill Gibbins.

In southern New South Wales the town of Holbrook looked at its history and created a tourist profile by placing a submarine in the main street. In Longreach, in central western Queensland, the town is overcoming the body blow it suffered a decade ago with the collapse of the wool reserve price scheme by also focusing on its heritage. Through the construction of the

Jamie McKew, co-founder of Port Fairy
Folk Festival, loves nothing more than to
join the playing at the festival. (Photo by
David Owen, courtesy of Jamie McKew)

Stockman's Hall of Fame, Longreach celebrates the lives and
deeds of Australians in the harshness of the Outback. It is the
spiritual home of the Outback. But it is not just Longreach that
has benefited from the Stockman's Hall of Fame. Towns like
Winton and Barcaldine have also received a boost and consequently focused on promoting their own history as tourist
attractions. It is a continuing process of renewal exemplified by
the Shear Outback project at Hay in the western Riverina,
involving the best of the old and the new from the shearing
industry in a hall of fame-style complex. This project was

officially opened on Australia Day 2002 and commemorates shearing, including the role of trade unions in the early days of the wool industry.

All of these developments underline the sense of renewal that is alive in the Outback—among people and communities that see stars and not bars. This book is the story of many of them. There are many, many more that deserve to be told and no doubt will, for inspiration and determination will reap their reward—even in the vastness that is the Outback.

The Drover's Way

ROGER FLETCHER

Roger Fletcher pulls up a plastic chair in the sparsely furnished staff kitchen that doubles as the boardroom at the Dubbo head-quarters of Fletcher International Exports and pushes a cup of Nescafé across the table. On the side of the cup is a message that encapsulates the philosophy of Australia's sheep king: 'Lift your expectations.' The message is one that he's been applying throughout his life and which often turns conventional wisdom on its head. In the process, it has laid the foundations for extra-ordinary growth in Dubbo, the biggest city of the New South Wales central west and gateway to the state's Outback.

For some years after Roger's high-tech abattoir opened in 1988, Dubbo was the fastest growing regional centre in Aus-tralia. After Coffs Harbour on the state's north coast, Dubbo has the second largest regional passenger airport in New South Wales, with several flights a day to capital cities. Population doubled in the two decades to 2001 when it stood at around 40,000. On any given night, though, the city's population could be as high as 44,000 due to the number of people passing through, driving road trains or visiting the open range Western Plains Zoo. In the central west, Dubbo acts like a magnet, drawing people to jobs that are no longer to be found in smaller outlying towns. It is the de facto capital city of a region with a population of more than 150,000 people.

Employing more than 700 people at the abattoir, Roger Fletcher was quick to see the advantages of Dubbo: it is a transport hub that sprawls around the intersection of the Mitchell and Newell highways, 416 kilometres west of Sydney, linking the New South Wales capital to Perth, and Brisbane to Melbourne. Dubbo, in the local Aboriginal language, means red earth. The area was explored by John Oxley in 1818 and settled by Europeans in 1824. The settlement grew originally around a store opened on the banks of the Macquarie River by Jean Serisier in 1841 and the village of Dubbo was proclaimed in 1849. The town became an important stopping place on the stock route south to Victoria. The city of Dubbo was proclaimed in 1966.

Many of the people who work for Roger Fletcher live in nearby towns such as Narromine and Wellington and commute daily. Others have moved to Dubbo to live. 'They may not be in their smaller communities but at least we've kept them in the bush rather than them going off to Sydney to get work,' Mayor Allan Smith says. 'Roger's had a big impact, not just on Dubbo but the region.' These days, the city extends along the Macquarie River. The highways, railway lines and stockyards are visible from the Fletcher house, which is situated on one of the few hills in the district, above the abattoir to the north of the city.

Pubs built in Dubbo's earlier days slake the thirst of the abattoir employees, as well as local farmhands and itinerant transport workers who help keep the city's industries humming.

There may be some brashness to be found on the streets of Dubbo, but there is little sulkiness, for this is a city that knows there are jobs for those who want them. The vibrant arts community which will help attract the doctors and lawyers— whose services are in demand in a rapidly growing city—may still be in the nurturing stage, but unemployment is below the national and state average at around only 5 per cent. Former Dubbo mayor Tony McGrane, now an Independent state MP, says Roger Fletcher has helped change the city's attitude through his success. 'No-one equals his vision,' McGrane says. 'It rubs off. Everybody here is a self-achiever. There is no old Establishment, no Old Money. There's a lot of wealth, it's all new money and young people, all willing to have a go.'

A big man standing 183 cm tall in size 11 boots, Roger Fletcher is tanned and solidly built. A ready smile and engaging blue eyes provide an interesting contrast to the cauliflower ears and flattened nose, broken in a fall off a pushbike as a child and further bent on the football field. It is the face of a survivor. Indeed, he played representative rugby league as a forward for New South Wales Northern Division and attracted the interest of Western Suburbs in Sydney but turned down an offer from the club, instead seeing a brighter future in the bush, turning sheep into mutton.

His beginnings were humble. 'I started with nothing and now have up to 1,200 people working for me,' Roger says proudly about his family-owned company which exports sheep meat, wool and anything else left over to 80 countries. It has been said that the only thing Roger Fletcher does not export is the bleat. He sends lips to South Africa and leg sinews to Korea, where both are chewed as a delicacy.

The journey that took Roger to Dubbo began on the stock routes of northern New South Wales and Queensland in the 1960s. But the values he honed on the endless 'long paddock' were first learnt in his childhood. He grew up in a big family on a poor farm at Glen Innes in northern New South Wales. He soon understood the merit of hard work and grabbing opportunities as they arose. Rabbits may have been a curse, but to young Roger they were a potential source of money. 'I was selling my own rabbits when I was strong enough to set rabbit traps,' he recalls. 'I'd say, "Mum, would you go and get the rabbit guy to buy my rabbits?" and she'd say, "They're your rabbits, you sell them". So I was trading when I was six or seven years old, getting five bob a pair.'

Roger's mother was a horse dealer and he learnt other valuable lessons from her about doing business—lessons that he has taken with him and applied throughout his life. 'She'd buy the horses and then she would look for the right customer who could handle that horse rather than finding the right horse for the rider. It's no good putting a real city kid on a three-year-old pony that's going to shy. That comes right back to marketing and it's what I do today. I don't look at the markets, I look at the products we've got and then say, "we've got this product, now we need to find a market for it".'

Roger left the Farrer Agricultural High School at Tamworth at fifteen. Five years later, in 1966, he left the family farm to go droving. He had $10,000 from his share in the farm, the clothes he stood up in, an old ute, a bit of netting to fence the sheep in, and half a dozen dogs. He saw opportunities in heading for wherever there was a drought. 'Where there's a loser, there's a winner,' Roger says in a simple homily that belies his astuteness. He would buy the sheep and walk them. To him, the economic benefits of being on the road were simple. 'I would get an irrigated farm by going to where the rain rains,' he says. 'I'd buy them where there was no grass and walk 'em towards grass. How much did the land cost me?—nothing. I only had so much money so I had to buy all the sheep I could. That means everything I had was in the sheep. I only had enough for 2,000. They had to grow wool. They had to make a profit.'

For Roger, the years of droving provided the education that would underpin his future business dealings. 'Think about it, if you can't solve problems when you're droving you're going to die. You've got to be a vet when the animals are crook, a doctor when someone gets crook, a weather forecaster, a solicitor able to argue with the cockies and the rangers when they're into you, a mechanic when the old truck breaks down, and your own accountant, cook and find a feed off the land. Most people who go to university don't learn any of that.'

He had no ties and home was where he unrolled his swag. Roger's easygoing manner meant he was able to talk his way out of most problems he encountered droving. However, there is one fight he admits to. It happened during the 1969 drought when he was the other side of Charleville on the Ward River while walking a mob from central Queensland to Glen Innes on an epic nine month journey. There had been some skullduggery by locals, ensuring the mob ahead had cleaned out the scarce feed along the stock route. There was no grass and he badly needed to find feed for his stock. On coming across a station with a good paddock, he drove them in. The station manager objected, so, 'I said to this bloke I was with, "You look after the sheep, I'll argue with the cockie, fight with him to wear him out and then leave". It was the only way we were going to get feed.' By the time the fight was over, there was no grass left in the paddock. The fight story conjures up images of an earlier era and is reminiscent of Banjo Paterson's tale of the drover Saltbush Bill, and his fight 'on the well-grassed plain in the regular prize ring style' with a new chum English jackaroo during a drought:

> Now the new chum fought for his honour's sake and the pride of
>   the English race,
> But the drover fought for his daily bread with a smile on his bearded
>   face;
> So he shifted ground, and he sparred for wind, and he made it a
>   lengthy mill,
> And from time to time as his scouts came in they whispered to Salt-
>   bush Bill—
> 'We have spread the sheep with a two-mile spread, and the grass it
>   is something grand;
> You must stick to him, Bill, for another round, for the pride of the
>   Overland'.

When journalist Peter Bowers drew Roger's attention to the Saltbush Bill story in 1993, it was the first he knew of it. He remains bemused by the story of Bill's resourcefulness and the similarity to his own experience . . .

Around the late 1960s, Roger started selling his sheep. He recalls meeting 'an old guy of the meat trade' in Glen Innes who offered to show him how to make some money. Roger listened. Instead of selling the sheep he started killing—about 300 sheep a week. It gave him a toehold in a lucrative industry, but one that was beset by problems of inefficient council control

Roger and Gail Fletcher, with their children Melissa and Farron, have worked hard to ensure the success of their abattoir and export business as well as Dubbo's growth as a regional centre. (Courtesy of the *Daily Liberal*, Dubbo)

and a union closed shop with work practices dating back generations.

Many of Roger's droving jobs terminated at Moree, where the stock would be sold and processed at the Moree Council abattoir. Over time, he struck up a friendship with a telephonist at the Moree exchange, Gail Allen. He invited her out, but she protested, saying he wouldn't want to take her out as she was Aboriginal. He persisted, and within a year they were married, with the union producing three children—Pamela, Melissa and Farron. Roger leased a farm and Gail took care of the books.

For the next decade, Roger did not make much money from his killing operations, but he worked hard and learnt the business. Gail directed the finances. People who have watched the Fletchers over the years say Roger did not do too much without first discussing it with Gail. This is as true today as it was then. Indeed, Roger says of his wife: 'She was the financial wizard. In the early days she did it all. The teamwork was fundamental.' Mayor Smith echoes this. 'He knows everything about the sheep and the stock; but Gail is the financial guru. She has been very much part of the whole thing and had a lot to do with the direction in which Roger has gone. Roger and Gail are a team.'

Roger Fletcher had half a dozen people working for him when a big flood devastated northern New South Wales in the early 1970s. He remembered that in his childhood the family had always collected the wool from dead sheep. 'When we were four and five years old we picked up all the dead wool at home,' he says. 'We would go round all the farms, my brother and me, picking up dead wool from sheep that had died in the drought. I learnt that dead wool was better than shorn wool because there are no second cuts and you get the full staple. Dad would bag the dead wool, sell it, and give some money to my brother and me. I always reckon that with every negative there's always a positive.' When the flood struck many sheep drowned, but rather than leave the carcasses to rot in the paddocks Roger took a small wool press out and collected the dead wool, just as had happened in his childhood. 'It kept my people employed,' he says. 'It looked like a tragedy, but it was no tragedy. We just went on from there. No-one picked up the dead wool until we did.'

The reaction from woolgrowers was antagonistic. Roger remembers that they treated him as a leper, demanding that he sell his fellmongered wool 'over there' because it was allegedly inferior. 'The buyers in their good wisdom would go and tell everyone it's no good and then buy as much as they could as cheap as they could,' he recounts. 'That's fair enough, I can accept that, that's gamesmanship.'

He remembers one particular day at the Dubbo plant when a visiting businessman who owned woollen mills in South America and England looked at the wool coming out of the fellmonger and said, 'I've never seen this in my life, this is incredible wool'. According to Roger, he looked out the window and said, 'Can I build a woollen mill over there?' But Roger Fletcher the loner has always made it his practice not to take partners. He replied, 'No, we don't work that way'. As the businessman walked off the plant Roger turned to a young worker and said, 'We're going to build a woollen mill over there'. 'Thirty million dollars later we had a woollen mill.'

But before Roger built a woollen mill he had to build an abattoir. By 1981 he had left Moree to establish boning facilities at council-owned abattoirs in two other New South Wales towns, Gunnedah and Mudgee. With old, uneconomic abattoirs around New South Wales closing, Roger approached the New South Wales Meat Industry Authority chairman, John Carter, to discuss the problem.

Roger knew that ownership was the only way he could add value to the product. He was considering buying the Cootamundra abattoir, but John Carter talked him out of it. Why not build a state-of-the-art abattoir at Dubbo? Carter was persuasive. Dubbo was the biggest sheep selling centre in Australia and a crossroads of national transport links. Roger quickly agreed. 'I walked out of his office covered in a deep sweat and said, "Jesus, how am I ever going to make it"?'

But he knew he had been offered a once in a lifetime opportunity. At Dubbo, everything was going for him: 'It was a decent-sized town for the workforce and there were good roads coming in. You didn't have to think about it—that's how long it took for me to make that decision and there was no turning back.'

At his first meeting with the Dubbo Council, Roger went straight to the point: he owed the council nothing and they owed him nothing. He offered to buy land on the northern outskirts of the city at market value and said that all he wanted was no hold-ups with building approvals. They reached agreement and the plant opened in 1988, the first new abattoir in Australia for twenty years. Since then, Roger has bought 600 hectares surrounding the works, allowing him to dispose of plant effluent which is collected in a series of dams. About 360 hectares are irrigated by spraying the effluent through centre-pivot irrigators, and this land is used either for hay production, crops or running livestock. As well, all salt washed out of the skin salting shed is captured in evaporation pits and not allowed to enter any waste water streams.

When he looked at modernising the industry, Roger decided to employ a fresh, young workforce that did not have the entrenched ideas or inflexible attitudes that had bedevilled the old council-run, union-controlled abattoirs. He negotiated a new pay deal to replace the piecework pay system, with a fixed hourly rate. Many of his managers were employed not long out of school and with no knowledge of the business. Roger's approach was to train staff on the job. The benefit was that it built loyalty, especially among staff who began so young. As Mayor Smith says, 'He's really keen on giving young people a go'. Roger aims not to bring in people from other companies. He believes that if workers 'come over easy to you they will go easy to others. My first employee was a drover, a rough

Prime Minister John Howard with Fletcher International Aboriginal trainees during a visit to Dubbo. (Courtesy of the *Daily Liberal*, Dubbo)

little kid from a rough joint, but I took him on. It is one of my proudest things that he's now got seven road trains.'

There is another important aspect to his employment strategy. At the abattoir, he runs training programs for young Aborigines, providing jobs for about 70, or 10 per cent of his workforce, under the guidance of a permanent Indigenous employment mentor. Training ranges from jobs as labourers and boners to plant operators. Young Aboriginal women are trained as receptionists. As Roger puts it, 'Everyone we can help helps drag the family through'.

Warren Mundine, Indigenous employment mentor at the Dubbo Chamber of Commerce, says the Fletchers have a strong commitment to the Aboriginal community, which in turn holds them in high regard. 'They didn't just build the plant up and forget about people,' he says. 'There would be very few industries in Australia that would have as high Aboriginal employment as they do.' Warren says Roger Fletcher is a demanding person. 'Roger and Gail never ask anyone to do anything that they don't do themselves. That puts a lot of pressure on people to perform. It's a great place to learn, and people develop a tremendous work ethic. It's tough out there, but at the end of the day if it wasn't successful and people didn't like it they wouldn't be lining up to work there.'

The plight of Afghan asylum seekers from the Woomera Detention Centre captured Roger's attention during 2001. At a time when they were being used as a political football, he decided to give the Afghans an opportunity. Like them, he knew what it was like to start from scratch. Fifty of them on three-year temporary protection visas were soon working for him, initially at his Albany abattoir, then in both Albany and Dubbo.

With his Indigenous and youth training programs already in operation, he had a framework within which they could work. He told his managers that despite a few initial language problems, he was determined to see his move succeed. Starting on take home pay of $400 a week, the Afghans' English quickly improved and they were soon among Roger's most reliable employees. 'I don't see colour,' Roger told *The Australian*. 'As long as everyone meets our criteria, does the job and gets on with their lives then I'm happy to employ them.'

Under Roger Fletcher, the abattoir industry in Australia has evolved to a new age of efficiency. That change means that Australia can competitively export meat to anywhere in the world. Fletcher International processes 40,000 sheep a week at Dubbo. He lays claim to probably operating the most vertically integrated abattoir in the world. 'There's 800 tonne of raw material that walks into our abattoirs a day, from hooves to wool to ears to gut to meat,' he says. 'We've got to find a home for it. It's all good quality.'

All the lamb and mutton is Halal slaughtered in the manner prescribed by Islamic law. Indeed, in the year 2000 Saudi Arabia was Fletcher International's number one market destination, with $15.5 million of meat exports. Japan was the second largest market ($13 million), followed by the United Kingdom ($10.8 million), China ($10.7 million), Taiwan ($10.4 million), Algeria ($10.1 million), South Africa ($10 million) and the United States ($8.7 million).

Fletcher International is also a major processor of wool by-products. Processing of the wool is monitored, from the fellmongery to the final product, ensuring wool that is free of contamination. As well, the company produces quality chamois, while the rendering department produces a range of products suitable for the pet food, stockfeed and cosmetic industries. The US pet food company, Ralston Purina, came to Dubbo because of work Fletcher International did in America with them. Ralston Purina built a new export pet food plant principally aimed at supplying the Asia–Pacific market. They employ up to 100 people and are looking to expand their investment. 'The saleyards brought us here, then we brought over Ralston Purina,' Roger says. 'Because of the abattoir, we built a woollen mill, so one thing is growing on another.' In the past few years, he's watched containers of wool tops departing Dubbo for the clothing mills of Mexico under a zero tariff deal that allows the clothes to be sold in the lucrative American market.

In all of this personal success, Roger Fletcher is an unashamed nationalist. 'People come to me and say, "Jesus, you're lucky", and I say, "Yep, I was born lucky, I was lucky to be born in Australia". And if I'm sitting near a foreigner who came to Australia to live, I say, "You were fairly lucky, you got to Australia".'

Roger may have a quirky view on luck, but luck has had little to do with his company's success. Instead, confidence in his vision, determination to meet goals, and teamwork with Gail have been the features that have governed the company's progress. He has thrived on competition, staying ahead of rivals and refusing to rest on his achievements. 'If we said we're going to sit still today and we're going to take it easy for the next three years, we'll take some money out and we're just going to cruise, within that time the opposition would be at our heels,' he says. 'There is always opposition. Once you stop the competition you don't go ahead.'

He recalls a home truth from his droving years when he travelled from district to district: 'You would come across a town and on this side there'd be progressive farmers. You'd see them moving. Then you would drive out to the other side of town and all the blokes there would go to the pub every night. You didn't have to know much to realise that none of those farmers were any good. I think you could have taken the best farmer from the one side of town and put him on the other side and he would change the others, to a degree. A progressive farmer can drag along others around him.'

Roger Fletcher is adamant about the meaning of this for Australia today: 'What we have got to do is get some more doers. By having the sort of social security system we've got it's dragging people back. Competition breeds excellence. This is one of the problems. There are a lot of people out there who want to compete but don't.' It is a lesson he applied fervently to

Dubbo: 'My theory is that when we built Dubbo, inflation was 10 per cent. We reckoned we had to get 10 per cent better every year to survive. It's the same with the woollen mill. Since we've set it up we've cut the costs dramatically and improved quality. We have to because we sell the wool to the spinning mill and they're putting in better spinning facilities. When the wool goes to them it has to be better so that they can spin it quicker.'

Saddened by the decline of communities in many towns in rural and regional Australia today, Roger's message to people is to be positive. He acknowledges the reality that these towns can no longer survive on farming as they used to. But he is adamant that people can change a town: 'I think the opportunities are still there. You've got to have a vision. You need people with a vision who can pick things up and make them go. The opportunities out there are probably the same, although it is difficult to further process certain commodities we've got when you're facing competition from overseas that's got cheap wages and no environmental problems. All those things make it very difficult for us. But we've still got cheap raw materials and Australians are good, smart workers. I think we undersell ourselves a lot.'

On this, as with other issues, Roger is a staunch defender of Dubbo. 'We've done our share for Dubbo, and Dubbo has been good to us,' he says. 'I will never forget what one guy said to me when we came here, "Oh, you may think you've got it right but there's one thing wrong—Dubbo people won't work". I said, "They've got two arms, two legs, they're Australians. We're the fittest nation in the world, so we should be the best workers. You mean to tell me they can't work?"' Fourteen years later he can boast: 'We've never had a strike here.'

But then, Roger Fletcher maintained control of his company and its work practices from the start. He implemented a tough but fair regime in an industry that was moribund and in need of a shake-up by somebody who was prepared to go it alone. The circumstances were right for someone like him. He believes there is one critical factor that contributed to his success: his status as a private company. That status is something he guards jealously.

He recalls a mid-1990s meeting involving then prime minister Paul Keating, ACTU secretary Bill Kelty, the heads of five major public companies as well as Richard Pratt, head of the privately owned company Visyboard, and himself. 'We were sitting there and the public companies were whingeing about superannuation, quick turnovers, moving the money and where they should do it,' Roger remembers. 'Keating said we should be going out with some vision and looking three years forward. Dick Pratt leant across to me and said, "If ever you think or hear a whisper I'm going public, get to Melbourne as quick as you can and tan my rump".'

Roger recounts the story to reiterate his belief that people in business have a much better chance if they remain a private company rather than going public. 'You can move so much quicker. You can have vision. Every person in Australia has got a vision but they don't pick up their visions. They don't do anything about it. One of the biggest problems with most Australians is that they are fixing up yesterday's problem. They come to work and say, "We've got a problem, we've got to fix what we were doing yesterday". They're not on top of that, they should have fixed that up yesterday. I mean, I get an idea and I'll chase it straight away. That's the important thing.'

From the long paddock to Dubbo, Roger Fletcher has never stopped chasing. Maybe it's because he's still 'just a drover' at heart.

On the Breadline

TOM O'TOOLE

Dickhead and shovel. That's what they called him. To Tom O'Toole, the best $23 he ever spent was to change his name from Toole. One little letter and an apostrophe not only gave him a new identity but also began the process of countering years of classroom failure and low self-worth. It was 1973 and he was a 21-year-old baker taking a first step in business with the purchase of a block of land at Wahgunyah on the Murray River. A new name went with it.

But it would take some years yet before Tom O'Toole began to feel at ease with himself. By the time he did, he had become not only Australia's most successful individual baker but was a sought-after motivational speaker on the celebrity events circuit in Australia and overseas. On stage, Tom O'Toole is a picture of animation, discarding his coat and tie as he frenetically uses the dais to deliver homilies that draw on his life experiences.

Most people, he believes, are too busy doing 'the ready, aim, aim, aim' without realising that they should start firing. 'When I tell people to take a risk some of them say they will when they're organised,' Tom says. 'But you're never going to be organised! You can't wait until you're organised—you've got to begin today if you want success tomorrow. And you've got to keep lifting the bar.'

With blue eyes that shine, and a moustache that complements a ready smile, Tom O'Toole has been described as 'John Cleese on speed'. He radiates energy. And that energy is lucrative. By 2001, the Beechworth Bakery was turning over a staggering $3 million a year—the largest of any stand-alone retail bakery in Australia. But, says Tom wryly: 'If you're going to Beechworth you're going out of your way. Not so long ago you only went there to visit your mad aunt in the mental institution or a relative in jail.' Beechworth was home to the mad, the bad, the sad and going nowhere.

Go there any Sunday these days and you'll find that the bakery is packed with people who have made the three-hour drive from Melbourne or travelled from nearby Albury-Wodonga and Wangaratta to lunch upstairs on the balcony while listening to a jazz band. Over both levels, there is seating for more than 300 people. Such is the bakery's popularity that it is not uncommon for it to take more than $10,000 over the counter on any Sunday as customers choose from the range of 250 pies, cakes and pastries baked fresh daily. More than 600,000 customers pass through the bakery's doors each year, providing jobs for about 65 staff.

While Tom O'Toole is reluctant to take all the credit for turning the town into the thriving tourist mecca it is today, the bakery nonetheless is often credited with the rebirth of

Tom and Christine O'Toole with staff outside the Beechworth Bakery. (Courtesy Tom O'Toole)

Beechworth—not to mention inspiring many other rural communities and businesses across Australia, New Zealand and South Africa. 'Anybody with a belief, conviction and commitment can change the world, let alone a town,' Tom says. 'I had a belief in my business. I didn't necessarily think of the town.'

More than 20,000 people lived in Beechworth in the 1850s before the gold petered out. Over the next century Beechworth increasingly depended on government institutional jobs. By the early 1980s, more than a third of the town's population of around 3,700 were either inmates, patients or employees at the prison, the district hospital, the hospital for the aged or the Mayday Hills psychiatric institution, which alone provided 500 jobs. From a vigorous regional centre it stagnated into a town dependent on government pay cheques and increasingly devoid of initiative.

Beechworth supermarket owner and Indigo Shire Councillor Andrew Banks has worked with Tom O'Toole through the town's chamber of commerce. He has no doubt that Tom gave the town a kick-start just when it was needed. 'Beechworth is a town that in many ways had it easy,' he says. 'It was a government town and this meant that the Great Depression of the 1930s never happened here. It had a background of security and became insular. But in the mid-1990s when Mayday Hills closed, it was in trouble. The town had to change. Tom came at a time when Beechworth needed a lead. He has always promoted the town as much as he has promoted his own business. He is passionate about the town just as he is about his business.'

All this from a kid who grew up in abject poverty at Tocumwal in southern New South Wales on the Murray River. Born in 1952, Tom was one of a family of three brothers and one sister whose home was an army tent with a dirt floor. He was the second youngest. His father, Christopher Toole, was an Irishman from poor farming stock stretching back generations at Ratoath, near Dublin. He fought against the English, was jailed and then came to Australia, where he worked as a horseman and rabbiter before becoming a civilian driver at the airfield at Tocumwal during World War II. He met Nona Saunders in a café where she worked at Yarrawonga. After they married he worked as a casual labourer on the railways.

Tom went to the Sacred Heart Primary School at Tocumwal. His parents could not afford to pay the meagre school fees and provided the nuns with produce instead. He hated living in poverty and wearing other people's hand-me-downs. When his shoes wore out, cardboard would be inserted in the soles to keep water out. 'We didn't have a bathroom at home and we'd stink,' he says. 'The nuns would wash us at school because we peed the bed and we went to school in the same clothes we slept in. We didn't know any different.' He recalls going to the health camp at Portsea, Victoria. 'When I got there, everybody had to strip down to their undies. But we didn't have undies. We never had toothbrushes. I always felt so inferior.' He learnt that it was often safer to avoid people. As a result, he lacked the social confidence of his peers. Even today he prefers to stay off the shop floor, away from the customers.

He passionately hated school, he learnt little and as he puts it, failed kindergarten, not even learning the alphabet and stopping at the times-two tables. He would daydream and draw pictures. He was a quiet kid, a loner who was frequently in trouble. At home, his mother was the disciplinarian as his father was a pacifist. At school, the nuns often punished him. 'For most of primary school I was locked up in a cupboard under the stage,' he recalls. 'Every kid who got locked in there would scream. But not me. The nuns would lock me in there and I would love it. It was dark and black and they would forget I was there.' By being locked up Tom avoided schoolwork. He could be in a world of his own. 'There was a little knot hole in the door, and I peered out through it. They'd leave me there through lunchtime—I loved it.'

He would disrupt the class by suddenly running across desks and jumping out the classroom window. He would regularly skip school, signing notes with his mother's name. Often, he would be down the river, fishing, swimming, building forts or pinching boats. He never played sport. At athletics carnivals in primary school he would always enter the sack race. 'I would get a sack, hop in it, get among the sports gear and just stay in the sack all day. I hated sport.' The teachers would order him to play cricket. 'We had this big hunk of wood to bang the stumps in the hard clay. One day I remember banging the stumps in and I slipped deliberately and threw it up in the air. Next thing the thing hit me in the head and split it open. I've still got the scar.' But it got him out of playing cricket that time.

When he got older and too big for the cupboard Tom was locked in the toolshed instead. 'Other kids would get in there and smash the door, but I'd be quite happy just to sit in there,' he remembers. 'They'd lock me in the library sometimes. I didn't read. I never destroyed anything, but they would just forget I was there.' He recalls that all students had to learn to use the telephone but he says the nuns did not bother to teach him. Tom repeated several years in primary school before he got 'too big for the desk' and went to high school.

'When I got to high school, all I could do was just rule up my page and put the heading up because I had no maths. I didn't do anything else—I was allowed to read comics in class—yet they would give me great marks. That's all I had to do because I had no basic idea of how to do anything. I was a dunce and it was terrible.' Sport was compulsory at high school but he still would not play. 'I would refuse to bring my sports gear, so the headmaster would punish me. I had to take my shoes off and they would make me run around the oval where there were all these bindies. But I was brought up without shoes, so it didn't worry me. Then they'd get me in the car park, give me a bucket and I'd have to go and pick up every white stone, fill it up and take it back to the headmaster. Then he'd get the bucket and fling it all over the car park and I'd have to do it again. I did that every week.'

At fourteen, without completing the School Certificate, he left school and took a job in the local cordial factory, where he had worked casually during school holidays. He spent two years at the factory doing the jobs no-one else would do, before deciding to focus on his future by starting an apprenticeship. But his first choice, the butcher, did not want him. He decided to try and be an electrician but the local electrician said he would never make it with his poor education. That left the bakery, where a vacancy came up after the apprentice left. His father warned him that the baker was a hard man but he took the job anyway.

It was the era of big companies buying up small bakeries in country towns and closing them in order to use the premises as depots for their own product. When the baker sold Tom had to move to Shepparton to continue his apprenticeship. From Shepparton his employer sent him to Beechworth, where he worked at the Baker Boy Bakery—not far from the Ideal Café & Milk Bar that would ultimately become the Beechworth Bakery. In reality, the bakery was little more than a wholesaler. Beechworth became his home. He liked living there, despite the run-down state of the shops. He earned $15 a week and paid $12 in board for living on the premises. This meant he could not afford to drive his car all that far. By the time he was seventeen Tom was acting production manager. After eleven months at Beechworth he took a job at Albury.

Tom knew he wanted to make a lot of money. At nineteen, he says he was focused on success and knew that the first step to achieving this was a well-paid job. He began to set goals, intent on saving hard to overcome the poverty he had grown up with as well as his lack of education. While at Albury he heard of a new bakery that was being established at the Aboriginal settlement of Maningrida, in Arnhem Land. Copying from someone else's job application, he applied for the manager's job in 1972 and was successful.

The $6,000 a year that the job paid gave Tom a sense of self-worth and he began to like being a baker. He saw that the Maningrida Bakery was a cornerstone of the community. He was respected and accepted by the people. Over the next fifteen months he saved $10,000. He decided to put it towards buying a bakery back home at Yarrawonga, near Albury.

But the Yarrawonga business was hard going because of poor equipment, low prices and restrictions on what he could sell. The previous owner had signed an agreement with a baking chain that prevented him from producing sliced bread. Still, with 3,500 residents and 20,000 tourists a year—all with money to spend on cakes from his shop—he knew there was potential to make money. The problem was he did not know how to tap this potential. He knew nothing about advertising or promotion; he just opened the doors and hoped people would come in and buy. They stayed away.

Tom had returned from Arnhem Land with greater self-confidence, but he still found it difficult to mix in society, whether at the local Catholic church or the pub. He began reading Norman Vincent Peale's *The Power of Positive Thinking*. 'I couldn't run one bakery, but I got so positive after reading that book that I wanted to buy another one,' Tom says. He tried to sell Yarrawonga, but couldn't. Nonetheless, when he heard that a friend from his Beechworth days, Keith McIntosh, wanted to sell the Ideal Café, he decided to buy it—even though he had no money left. 'No bank would give me a loan to buy the business, so Keith's mother loaned me the money to buy it,' he says. Until he sold the Yarrawonga bakery, Tom would drive between the two businesses, carrying all his papers in a cardboard box. 'Then my car blew up so I hitchhiked between the two of them.'

Cradled in the foothills of the Australian Alps, Beechworth's wide tree-lined streets and solid dignified buildings are a reminder of the bustling goldrush days when the streets rang with the clamour and excitement of the quest for riches. More than four million ounces of gold—115 tonnes or approximately $2 billion worth (1997 prices)—were found in the first fourteen years after its discovery in 1852.

From the wealth created by the gold, Beechworth became the administrative centre for the region; the impressive architecture of the post office, town hall, library, hospital and prison reflecting its importance. The town was closely associated with Ned Kelly and his gang. In his younger days the bushranger spent time in the Beechworth Gaol. After he was captured in the last-stand shoot-out at Glenrowan, Kelly was sent to Beechworth, charged with the murder of two policemen at Stringybark Creek and remanded for trial. An impartial jury proving impossible to find, Kelly was transferred to Melbourne, where he was convicted of murder and hanged in 1880.

Tom had always liked Beechworth, having panned for gold in the streams over the years. The notion of 'gold in them hills' took hold. With his sister Betty and her husband, Allan Friar, who were partners in the business, they built it up and changed the name to the Beechworth Bakery and Milk Bar. Tom ran the bakery while Allan and Betty took care of the counter and the books. One of the reasons he reckons he felt at home in Beechworth was because of the mental asylum, whose patients would often wander into the bakery. He no longer felt he was the only misfit.

Three years after returning to Beechworth, and by now married, Tom decided to sell up and leave the town. He was working too hard and needed a break. His in-laws lived in Western Australia, which is where Tom and his wife ended up after starting to ride around Australia by pushbike. An opportunity arose to buy a bakery at Augusta in Western Australia's south-western corner.

Tom bought the business, only to find that the previous owner was telling everyone he would go broke within six months. But Tom had different ideas. 'In the first year I tripled his figures,' Tom says. 'How did I do it? The previous owner would do a third of a tray of cakes, or a half tray. I did full trays. I'm good at judging quantity and I knew the market was there. All he had to do was get out of the bakehouse and have a look at what's around. Years ago, most bakeries would be empty by just after lunch, but I always made sure I had plenty of product in the shop right up until I closed.' To Tom, the former owner was just 'another dream-taker'. He knew he didn't like dream-takers.

It was while in Western Australia that Tom began to travel and understand the potential of tourism. Southeast Asia, Malaysia, Norfolk Island, Mauritius, New Zealand and finally Europe opened his eyes to the market power that was waiting to be tapped. After returning to Beechworth to visit Betty and Allan, he saw the town with fresh eyes. He realised that with its colonial buildings it just might work as a tourist venue.

He sold up and went back to Beechworth with his head full of ideas and wanting to buy back the bakery that he had sold six and a half years earlier. The bakery was bankrupt, full of mice and rats and had a possum living in the bakehouse that ate the vegetables for the pasties. 'There was a health order on the place and it was going to close, but I wanted to buy it because I saw the potential of the tourist dollar. I went to my bank manager who said, "You're bloody mad. This town is dying". I changed banks.'

The renewed commitment to the bakery suited Tom's state of mind. He worked at night and slept during the day. Such a lifestyle allowed him a form of escapism. He admits he had become a workaholic. 'I would do two shifts every day, I'd work in the morning, have a sleep and come back in the afternoon and do another shift,' he says.

As he threw himself more and more into work at the bakery, his marriage was collapsing. Within six months of returning to Beechworth it was over. 'My wife left me and I wanted to die,' he says. The end came with a traumatic argument in which Tom contemplated suicide. 'If you ever want to stick a loaded gun in your mouth, they taste cold and oily. I didn't pull the trigger because my gun wasn't registered and I didn't want to get my wife into trouble. I got my wife to come with me and register the gun.' Tom thinks she thought he was going to shoot her. Next day she left. He mainly blames himself for the break-up, conceding his life was out of balance. 'I was not sane. Sane people don't put guns in their mouths.'

Now with the responsibility for raising two daughters, he realised he had to change. 'In every disaster lies an opportunity. I had to do the biggest investment in my life, I had to start investing in me.' Slowly, Tom got his life back in order. He reckons he became an easier boss to work with as he stopped yelling at his staff. He began to focus on what he really wanted for the bakery and for himself. He wrote out his goals on paper, bought new equipment and did a lot of self-analysis about who Tom O'Toole really was. He asked himself the question of

Tom and Christine O'Toole not only encourage their staff, but have motivated the rest of Beechworth to ensure that it is no longer a place for only 'the mad, the bad, the sad and going nowhere'. (Courtesy Tom O'Toole)

whether he wanted to be 'just a baker'. He decided to make a full-on commitment. Plans were drawn up and the bakery expanded in a frenzy of building activity.

But he was still a single father. That changed when a girl-friend from his earlier days in Beechworth, Christine McAnanly, came into the shop one day. A brown-eyed brunette, Christine had grown up in Beechworth in a Housing Commission home. Compared with Tom's childhood, hers was relatively comfort-able. For a start, she always had shoes. 'He had it a bit harder than the rest of us,' Christine observes.

In August 1986 they married. Suddenly there was stability in Tom's life—something he was not used to. 'Christine's calm and cautious, she's probably a realist and I'm a dreamer,' Tom says. 'Most of the time she balances me.' Christine sees Tom as more daring, possessed by drive and confident of his ideas whereas she is much quieter. 'I try to hold him back,' she says. 'At times it's gone a bit fine. I tend to be more the worrier; he's not. Tom always says he doesn't have to stress or worry because I do it for both of us. In the end I usually go along with him. But I don't always make it easy for him.' Importantly, the combination of daring and caution has jelled into a vital and successful relationship.

The bakery grew quickly. Tom bought the drapers next door and knocked down the dividing wall to open it up into the existing shop, doubling the floor space and entrances for customers. He extended the production and baking areas at the rear, while seating was extended to the footpath outside. The second storey and balcony were opened to the public in 1992 and a BYO liquor licence granted for these areas. 'Smell fans' were installed to blow smells from the ovens into the street. 'People sitting outside think, "I'll have another one of them",' Tom says. 'When we burn something we've got to turn the buggers off real quick.'

Through such wiliness the mood of the town began to change. From the 1950s many shops had been closed and a sense of resignation permeated Beechworth. 'Buildings were boarded up and people were living in the shops when I came here,' Tom recalls. 'Shops across the road were boarded up. The lolly shop was a funeral parlour, boarded up and used every now and then. I came in, started pulling down balconies and spending money. People told me I was mad. They reckoned we had created a monster and would never fill it. Our place isn't big enough now and many shops have now been renovated since we did ours.'

Tom saw his critics as dream-takers and not dream-makers—
'like bank managers and accountants, and sometimes we're
married to them'.

When he first opened he recalls going to bed with 'a can of
worms in my head and a football of fear in my guts', wondering
whether the customers would continue to come in. He invited
people to send in their comments and used them to help the
business expand. He still does so, and about 200 comment forms
a month are returned. 'They said they wanted tables and chairs
so I bought them and the people wanted more. I got the
people upstairs by putting the toilets upstairs.' One of the more
common complaints is that people are irritated by having to
wait to be served. But Tom refuses to introduce a 'numbers
system' at the counter because he doesn't want his customers to
be regarded just as a number. 'They're all people,' he says, 'not
a number.' Tom pins a current selection of customers' comments
on the bakery noticeboard for all to read—even the negative
ones.

Tom uses the comments to motivate his staff to provide 'that
little bit extra' in the service they give customers. 'I ask my staff
to improve 1 per cent a week.' His business, he says, is 5 per cent
technology and 95 per cent psychology. 'I believe business is so
simple,' he says. 'All the people want you to do is look at me,
greet me, talk to me and thank me. Lots of people do not look
at you.' He relates how he had a few hours to kill before a
speech in a Queensland tourist resort and visited the shopping
area. 'I watched for who gave me eye contact. Out of the eight
shops I went in, only one gave me eye contact. Lots of them
said "thank you" but they were looking out the window or at
their mate. It still happens here, but I keep telling my staff it's

the little things that make the big difference. Yet we're all out there looking for the big fix.'

To Tom, the attitude of his staff is all-important. He places inspirational posters throughout the bakery, undertakes regular staff customer service training, recognises staff initiatives, and organises staff meetings to determine policy and practice. 'People often forget about the staff,' he says. 'They get so tied up with data and spreadsheets. If I have happy staff I have happy customers and the money will pour in.'

He believes that to develop a vision people have to go beyond their own backyards. He sends his staff to other bakeries for experience and to conferences in Australia and overseas so that they can learn. He wants them to get out of their 'comfort zone'—as he did in 2000 when he was at a conference in New Zealand and he was challenged by everyone present to bungee jump. 'No way,' he replied, but then realised that to be honest with himself he had to have a go. A numbed Christine watched as the instructors trussed her husband up. He recalls her muttering something about whether his false teeth would be all right. He asked the instructors, who thought it was the funniest thing they had ever heard. With his mind in neutral, Tom made the leap, at first terrified and then exhilarated. And he kept his teeth. 'The greatest sin is sitting on your arse,' he says. 'You've got to go out there and beat your own bloody drum yourself. No-one else is going to do it for you. Be part of your community—stick your hand up and get involved.'

Together with a host of national and state business and customer service awards, the bakery has won the Victorian Tourism Award for Significant Regional Attraction on three occasions. Beechworth has become a major tourism centre that is expanding in population and employment opportunities and becoming a more diverse economy.

The Chamber of Commerce with the support of the Indigo Council has worked to help revive the town's fortunes. Among initiatives have been events such as the Celtic Festival, Drive Back in Time Festival, Golden Horseshoe Festival and the Harvest Festival. These festivals are providing yet another incentive to visit Beechworth. A recognition that there had to be a change of attitude as the town faced up to—and moved on from—the mentality of the government pay cheque helped to pull Beechworth through the gloomy period of public sector rationalisation. As Tom sees it, the town matured from its long-held attitude that tourists were 'terrorists and rubber necks'. 'They realise that without the tourist dollar today, their kids are going to have to leave the town.'

In 2001, Tom took his philosophy one step further. He and Christine sold part of the business to four employees—his daughter from his first marriage, Sharon, and three long-term employees. As the business continued to grow, Tom realised that he could no longer expect to run it on his own. In September 2001 the new company—in which Tom and Christine retain a majority shareholding—bought the Drover's Bakehouse at the historic Murray River port town of Echuca. It might have been a new, specially designed $3 million bakery, but it was struggling. Under the weight of mounting losses, the owners faced the prospect of closing the bakery's doors. Tom saw an opportunity for himself and his staff.

Yet in the face of such entrepreneurial flair, traces of the old Tom remain. On the day the new bakery opened, a Bendigo baker came in. Tom was out the back doing the dishes, preferring the anonymity of the kitchen: 'you don't have to use a lot of brainpower washing dishes'. The baker recognised Tom, and of course wanted to meet him. There is an irony in Tom avoiding such meetings in his bakeries. Even today he rarely goes front of house. Yet in front of an audience he changes into an inspirational speaker who can talk without drawing breath, holding those present captivated by the forcefulness of his message.

On such occasions the old Tom Toole becomes the new Tom O'Toole. He motivates people by giving them glimpses of his life. The lessons he has learnt the hard way have been the most valuable. And they started early. As a five-year-old, he proudly rode his pushbike up the main street of Tocumwal, hitting a silent cop and falling off. 'I made a real dick of myself but I got back on. Falling off my bike was part of learning. So is life. You've got to keep getting back on that bike.'

Tom has, again and again.

Go West, Young Woman

MELISSA FLETCHER

Melissa Fletcher-Toovey spent her school holidays in an abattoir, working unpaid double shifts. She was thirteen when she started, taking on tasks like paying the workers or organising export shipments. Melissa wanted to impress her father, sheepmeat king Roger Fletcher. A few years earlier, she told Roger she wanted to be a movie star when she grew up, but added, 'If I can't do that I want to have your job and be boss'. One way or another, there's always been a special bond between Melissa and Roger.

Born in Moree, New South Wales in 1975, Melissa went to primary school in Gunnedah before boarding at Presbyterian Ladies College in Armidale. She recalls that when she was in Year 11 another girl won an exchange student scholarship to the USA. Melissa applied for the program herself by forging her parents' signatures. On acceptance, she then had the task of convincing them to allow her to go to Alabama.

She returned more independent. She found the lifestyle in the

American south challenging. A part-Aboriginal student at an all-white school, she encountered racism. She had many arguments, encouraging a less racist attitude among school friends and helping some to befriend Afro-Americans. The experience helped shape her credo that people should treat others as they find them. 'Don't generalise or keep people in a stereotype or group,' she once told the *Albany Advertiser*. Like her father, she sees 'good and bad in every race . . . don't prejudge people or put them in boxes,' she says.

Returning to Australia, Melissa finished Year 12 and won a place at Sydney University to study psychology and social work. But Roger convinced her to defer for a year and work in the company. She did and never took up the university offer. At nineteen, Melissa studied for the diploma of meat management in Melbourne. The course ran for three months each year over three years. As the youngest person and the first woman to apply, she experienced some difficulty being accepted into the course. But in the end, she finished second in the class and narrowly missed out on being dux.

From the contacts she developed during the course she learnt what the industry's problems were, providing invaluable experience when Fletcher International decided to build a plant near Albany, Western Australia. Albany's location caught Roger Fletcher's eye. He was looking to expand his sheepmeat processing empire and reasoned that Albany was ideally placed. Not only was it a long-established sheep region, but it was located close to major shipping routes.

Fletcher International built a new $45 million abattoir on a green-fields site in Narrikup, outside Albany. Melissa was part of the team of nine from Dubbo—all of them under 25 years of age—who started up the Albany abattoir in June 1998. Roger Fletcher hired an outsider as plant manager, but he did not last and Melissa soon took over. 'By the time Dad got over I was the plant manager, which I wanted to be,' she says. 'Otherwise, I don't think I would have got the opportunity.

Everything fate-wise went well for us. Our little team didn't know much but we learnt quick. We had the faith.'

By the end of the second week she had hired 60 staff. None of them had any abattoir experience. They did not know how to sharpen a knife, let alone cope with the sight of blood on a slaughterhouse floor. Melissa showed them how to do the job. She may be the boss, but she too works in the killingroom and takes her turn keeping the floors clean.

Melissa saw Narrikup as an opportunity to implement a different management and workforce style in quest of her goal to better Dubbo's production targets. She secured agreement from her staff to work an hour longer each day than their counterparts in Dubbo. After less than two and a half years she had reached her goal, processing about 45,000 sheep a week compared with about 40,000 a week in Dubbo.

Her emphasis has been on building teamwork and breaking down hierarchy. 'I knew as a girl coming in to work in school holidays that there was a definite pecking order. It's through the whole industry. I wanted things to change, with people working more together. I don't believe in staff car parking, so it's first in best dressed. I am a unitary sort of person; I like it to be together. I believe in staff and supervisors all dressing the same. The best pair of shoes I've got is a pair of gumboots, and everyone can swear to that, they see me running into Woolies with my gumboots on. Your vanity gets lost when you wear gumboots and a hairnet every day.'

Workers are employed on individual workplace agreements. New employees are put on probation for two months and paid an hourly rate while they learn. The result is a system different from any other abattoir in Australia. 'The whole plant's employees in all divisions are multi-skilled. For example, the slaughter floor—75 people—can do every job; everyone is multi-skilled,' Melissa says. 'There is no "I'm better than you", or fear of missing out on bonuses. It took a little bit longer but now it's starting to pay dividends, because people are proud of them-selves, as they learn each job and become part of the team. I've got women who are on the same money as men as they do the same jobs. I had to fight with Dad quite a bit, but we got through a system where we're a team.' Two things jump out when watching workers in this state-of-the-art abattoir. First is their speed of action. Second is their demeanour, as this is not a sullen workforce.

She learnt the importance of this interdependence from her parents, whom she says never stopped working as she and her sister and brother grew up. Her mother Gail was a critical influence. 'She grounded us, she filled in all the gaps—she played mum and dad for us. Dad taught us to open the gates, fix fences and round up sheep. Mum taught us many basic things that other kids get from their father—like how to throw and catch a ball. These were the sacrifices.'

Sacrifices there may have been, but Melissa and her brother and sister learnt a strong work ethic. 'Dad's never been someone that's ever stood back from something,' Melissa says. 'You see a problem you jump in and give a hand; don't matter who you are or how dirty you get. That's how we've all learnt the same. There were times when Dad never stopped.'

Melissa recalls her father saying how he was on the verge of bank-ruptcy and fighting the stock agents the day she was born. His words fell on deaf ears until the Agents' Association manager's secretary walked into the meeting to tell Roger that his wife had given birth to a daughter. It broke the ice and Roger got the credit terms needed to survive.

'The big thing I have learnt from him is to always be willing to take a chance; always look to improve and don't ever accept that if a thing is going well it's right,' she says. 'You've always got to get that one step better. That's something we've absolutely instilled in the culture of our people.'

For her part, Melissa is one of the few original staff from Dubbo still at Narrikup. Her one big regret has been the impact of a severe drought in 2001 that forced her to lay off more than 160 of the plant's 470 workers and operate a single shift daily. 'That was the hardest six months of my life,' she says. 'It was heartbreaking. I won't lie to you, there are days when you think you can't do it, times when you get down but you never give up.'

The daughter of the father whose motto is 'lift your expectations' has learnt her lessons well.

Different Folks

JANE BENNETT

The kids from the valleys were different. Every day, from the backwoods they would emerge, out of the Kombis and hippie housing dotted among the forests of northern Tasmania. They didn't look like the other kids at school, didn't fit in and were often ostracised.

Jane Bennett remembers that growing up in Tasmania in the 1970s was not easy for anyone who was different. Not that she was an 'alternative'. But she never shunned them, for she was attracted by what they represented. Here were kids who came from families who saw the world from a different perspective and had radical attitudes—as well as their way-out clothes. Many of Jane's neighbours regarded the newcomers as a threat to the way of life that had gone on in Tasmania for generations, but Jane was comfortable with a new way of thinking.

After all, from childhood, she could turn her hand to almost anything on the family dairy farm. So much so that she was her father's 'right hand man'. These days she can afford to be whimsical about it: 'When my first brother was born, a neighbour said to Dad, "You must be glad you've got a son at last". I glared at him, but Dad just replied, "I don't need a son, I've got Jane". I learnt at the age of twelve that driving a tractor was easier than picking raspberries so I took up tractor driving and doing things like shifting irrigation pipes.'

Twenty years ago, when Jane Bennett was growing up in Elizabeth Town, a one-pub village on the outskirts of Deloraine, her community was facing social and economic upheaval. The Bennetts had farmed the area for generations, watching the community slowly decay and its residents become more eccentric.

Jane's mother Maureen used to collect for the Red Cross from one old farmer at his ramshackle house. 'Either he'd come to the door, and all the chooks and pigs would rush out or, as you headed for the door, they'd all try to beat you through,' Jane says. 'He couldn't work out why his pigs were dying every time they went near the fence, or why his beard sizzled when he went to have a look. Perhaps it had something to do with the 240 volts they were getting from the wire he'd flung over the mains to electrify the fence . . .'

Eventually death came to the old farmer, and his land along with other farms was subdivided. New families moved into the area. A community revival began, with some residents commuting to Devonport and Launceston and others becoming jewellers, potters, painters and furniture makers working from home in an area that has now changed from traditional farming and timber milling to a more diverse artisan economy.

Coinciding with this was an economic shake-out in the dairy

industry sparked by deregulation. Jane's uncle John Bennett had been president of the Australian Dairy Farmers Federation from 1976 to 1985 and deputy chairman of the Australian Dairy Corporation from 1981 to 1986. He had extensive knowledge of the industry and a clear understanding of the direction that dairying, particularly in Tasmania, was headed. John and Jane's father, Michael Bennett, had already begun thinking about the need to diversify the family dairy business.

They realised that farmers like them were just price-takers in an industry that was producing and selling commodity products subject to the vagaries of international markets and the value of the Australian dollar—they were told what they would be paid and would then have to cut costs accordingly. The trouble was, they were at the end of the production line and there was no-one left to squeeze. They became interested in making cheese as a means of regaining control. But they needed a cheesemaker—and Jane was the link.

The Bennetts established their company, Ashgrove Farm Cheese, at a time when the strategy of value adding and developing agricultural niche markets was in its infancy in Australia. Uncertain about the future viability of the dairy farm, Michael and Maureen Bennett took a trip to Europe in 1986 that was to profoundly change their thinking. They began to see an opportunity in cheese production beyond the relatively limited styles made in Australia. Jane recalls that they brought her back a present—an apron with cows all over it from a gruyère factory in Switzerland. 'Dad had decided that I was going to be a cheesemaker.' Jane was appalled at the idea and told her father that she would never make cheese. Ever.

She remembers thinking how uncool it would be. After all, there was the dreary white uniform and 'that hat'. But faced

The success of Ashgrove Farm Cheese has given Jane Bennett plenty to smile about. (Peter Rees)

with her father's 'dripping tap' technique of persuasion over the years she succumbed, and today Jane is one of the very few Australian female cheesemakers, running an expanding family business.

But she's never worn the apron.

Now in her early thirties, Jane is no longer a tomboy but tall and willowy, with her Celtic origins clearly evident in her black hair and blue eyes. As production manager for Ashgrove Farm Cheese, she believes most things are possible with a will and some lateral thinking. This philosophy was nurtured while working on the family property and reinforced during the time she learnt cheesemaking.

It has also influenced her stance and perceptions as a community leader and the insights which she brings to her appointments to various state and national committees. Among these, she has become president of the Tasmanian Rural Industry Training Board, a member of the boards of the Rural Training Council of Australia, the Tasmanian Board of Agricultural Education, the Tasmanian Food Industry Council and the Tasmanian Electronic Commerce Centre. Between May 1999 and March 2000 she was a panel member of the Federal Government's Rural Transaction Centre Advisory Panel, followed by another appointment over the next six months as a panel member of the Government's Telecommunications Service Inquiry.

Her success has won her the titles of ABC Radio Tasmanian Rural Woman of the Year and ABC Radio Australian Rural Woman of the Year, both in 1997. The following year she won the National Regional Development Award in the Young Australian of the Year Awards. But it's not just her gender that has marked Jane Bennett as an achiever in a traditionally male-dominated industry. She has won recognition for her contribution to agriculture and to the economic development of her region. In 1995 she won the George Wade Medal for services to agriculture from a young person.

'One of the big things for communities in rural and regional Australia is that if we are going to survive we have to re-invent ourselves because agriculture is not going to be anybody's saviour,' Jane says. 'Farms will become bigger and more automated, farmers less likely to employ full-time labour and far more likely to employ itinerant contractors.' With mines having limited lifetimes and employment from forestry decreasing, Jane contends that finding new enterprises in new areas will be the only answer for many people.

Indeed, the growth of Ashgrove Farm Cheese is indicative of the way Deloraine has faced up to the changes forced on Australian rural communities by economic uncertainty and increasing mechanisation of agricultural and timber industries. The impact of these changes in the past two decades has seen youth unemployment in the area at a high 16 per cent. As elsewhere in rural areas, jobs were lost and a demoralised mood developed, replacing the economic and social certainty that for decades had guided the lives of people in these districts.

In 1990, there was another setback when Deloraine was bypassed by Highway One. Twelve businesses closed. Jane, her family and leaders of the Deloraine community realised that they had to do things differently if they were to find jobs, strengthen social cohesiveness and survive. The key was to rethink how to use existing resources. In the case of Jane's family, it was taking milk from the century-old dairy farm and processing it in a way that would fill a gap they'd identified in the market— English-style cheese.

While the Bennetts diversified into cheese, another nearby dairy began growing and processing raspberries, including dried raspberries, arrestingly marketed as 'Lust Dust' through their own cafe. Yet other farmers around Deloraine have begun harvesting the European delicacy, truffles, which are so good they have attracted the interest of the French—as well as local bandicoots.

Deloraine is the centre of a picturesque rural community that nestles in a fertile valley of the Meander River dominated by Quamby Bluff and the majestic Western Tiers. Situated exactly halfway between Launceston and Devonport on the Bass Highway, it traces its history back to 1823 when Governor Sorell ordered exploration further west from what is now the Longford district, to find suitable agricultural land. The area was named Deloraine, after Sir William Deloraine in Sir Walter Scott's poem 'Lay of the Last Minstrel'.

Jane Bennett learnt cheesemaking in a male-dominated profession. In 1986 she left school and returned to the family farm to work. Two years later in 1988, she enrolled at Gilbert Chandler, the Werribee-based Dairy Technology College for Australia. She was the only girl in a class of eighteen. The college worked on a system whereby dairy companies selected the employees who showed potential. After completing the college course, they returned to their companies as supervisors or factory managers. Jane was the first student not to have such an industry background, to have zero knowledge of the dairy processing industry. 'I was on an immensely steep learning curve in an alien, all-male environment,' she says.

Often the butt of jokes, she nonetheless was accepted by her male colleagues. 'They said to me at the end of the two years that I hadn't tried to be too girly-girl and that was why I fitted in and worked so well with them. They'd mostly forget that I was a girl and we'd go off to Melbourne, seven men and me and we'd get these funny looks. Even I could forget I was a girl.'

The course involved spending time working in the industry, but as Jane did not have a company to go back to she approached United Milk Tasmania and was offered a job. 'They knew what we were up to, that we were intending to build a cheese factory,' she says. 'But like everybody else, they thought it was a bit of a joke, so they weren't at all worried.' Jane went to the company's factory in Wynyard, near Burnie, for six months and gained experience cheesemaking. The company offered her a permanent position and to pay for her second year at college, but she declined. Jane reasoned that to do so would be unfair. 'I knew there was no value in that because I needed a good relationship with them when I built the cheese factory.'

Graduating with the Advanced Certificate in Dairy Technology, Jane returned home to be told by her father she could go to England to learn small farm cheesemaking. But there was a catch—she had to fund her own trip and that meant working nine months on the farm to pay for the fare. Three weeks after her twenty-first birthday she flew to England, taking up a position with Butlers' Farm House Cheese, a small factory in the Lancashire hills. She soon found herself writing a quality assurance (QA) program for the company. With contracts for supermarkets, including Sainsburys and Tescos, requiring a QA program and no other employees having the experience, Jane became quality control manager.

A few weeks into her employment with Butlers, she also became the resident Lancashire cheesemaker with the company, and pioneered the technology of direct vat inoculation of starter culture as opposed to the more unreliable traditional methods of making culture. 'I was making cheese, packing cheese, product development, dabbling in everything,' Jane says. 'I went from making cheese at Wynyard, where I was just a cog in a wheel, to where I had all this freedom. I would invent jobs. That was where I found my forte. Butlers were incredibly generous in allowing me to do so much and encouraging me to gain experience in so many areas of the business. The edge I had gained at Werribee gave me the advantage over all the English cheesemakers, but in turn I was able to bring home the UK technology in packaging and marketing, especially with supermarkets.'

This knowledge meant Ashgrove had a QA program from day one. It also meant their products were well-received in supermarkets around Australia. These were valuable volume

The milk provided by these peacefully grazing cows can be found as cheese in supermarkets all over the country. (Courtesy Jane Bennett/Ashgrove Farm Cheese)

markets that helped increase the company's output and offset the enormous capital expenditure of the operation.

While Jane was busy making cheese in England, Michael and his brother John were preparing to construct the factory. They scoured the country for second-hand equipment. Upon Jane's return, the family set about planning the cheese factory. There were no such factories in Tasmania and Jane had to start from the ground up. She even assembled the pasteurising machine herself as she could not afford to send all the plates over to Melbourne to be cleaned and fitted with new gaskets. 'We did it up, turned it on and it leaked like a sieve,' she remembers. 'Dad and John were standing there, yelling "Wind it up, wind it up". I was hanging off this spanner until I had it tight enough so that it worked. It was the best learning experience as I know in intricate detail how a pasteuriser works. It was just terrifying, though.'

While Jane was still overseas Michael and John applied for a farmhouse cheese licence. As this was the first application for a licence that exceeded the 30-ton limit set in the 1940s it took more than a year to complete the bureaucratic process. The irony was that by the time the Bennetts actually started making cheese the industry had been deregulated and they could make as much cheese as they liked. Production began in November 1993 when Michael Bennett told his daughter he would deliver 2,000 litres of milk the next day. This forced Jane to stop procrastinating and get down to business.

She decided the first batch would be Lancashire as it was a style she was familiar with. 'I turned on the pasteuriser and it was all over in a few minutes as it was a 15,000 litre an hour unit,' she recalls. 'I was completely amazed but it was edible. I became quite sentimentally attached to the first batch for quite a while but I have never been so terrified in my life. I look back now and wonder how I did it. I was like a maniac for the first two weeks, I wouldn't let anybody help me. Then I realised it was possible to let other people do things.'

According to Jane, it was her father and uncle who had the vision. She maintains that without their resolve and commitment she never would have built a cheese factory, let alone become a cheesemaker. 'They were the ones with the passion and the drive. My involvement was completely accidental, it happened along the way,' she says. Michael Bennett sees her involvement in this way: 'Jane left school and she wasn't too sure what she was going to do. She had an inclination to be a teacher, but decided to have a year on the farm and loved it. During this time we talked about cheesemaking.' Michael Bennett is nothing if not understated.

He had been to England a few times over the years, the first occasion as a Nuffield Scholar when he looked at agricultural enterprises. On returning to England in 1985 he again looked at the potential of making English-style cheese in Tasmania. He concluded that it would need family commitment because the cheesemaker would have to be on top of every aspect, unlike in a company operation where there were experts at all the different production stages.

Watching Jane grow up on the farm, he always had faith that she could do and was prepared to do any task. He had long believed in her ability and he sensed in her a certain determination to see things through. Michael Bennett created the environment within which his daughter was to flourish. While Jane is the confident extrovert and his brother John more forthright, Michael is the quiet, somewhat introverted organiser and mentor. The combination has clicked.

Jane has always been an achiever. Her involvement with the Tasmanian Rural Industry Training Board was an early example of taking an opportunity when it appeared. She was on the committee as rural youth delegate for three years before being offered, and accepting, the board presidency in September 1996. To Jane, these programs are crucial as they are the only way to advance employment opportunities for rural youth.

It was a problem Jane pondered increasingly as she grew up in an area that since the early nineteenth century had been inhabited by farmers and timberworkers. By the late twentieth century however, the job certainty that these industries had offered generations of Tasmanians was under threat. Adding to the changing dynamics was an influx of people wanting to live alternative lifestyles who were drawn to the area by the beauty of the Meander Valley and the cheap cost of living. Many came from the mainland.

From the mid-1970s these changes saw jobs disappear and social tensions rise. It was a divided community, marked by an attitude of suspicion and, indeed, resentment. The hippies frequented their own shops and drank in their own pub. 'There was a real "them and us" attitude in the town,' Jane recalls. 'There were a lot of people who moved in—alternative lifestylers, hippies. They moved into the bush areas, lived in buses, Kombi vans, built their own houses, and became self-sufficient.'

This prompted strong reactions. Locals recall some Meander boys blowing up the bridge into Jacky's Marsh so the hippies could not get out to vote in one election. When Jane was at high school her best friend in Year 10 was a girl who had grown up in a bus in another alternative lifestyle stronghold, Golden Valley. Her parents were some of the district's original hippies. 'She was laughed at throughout school. She was one of the real outcasts when we were at school,' Jane says.

But in high school in the early 1980s this began to change, for the children of the original folk as well as those of the newer bush inhabitants realised they had the common problem of finding a job after leaving school. By the time Jane entered Year 10 she recalls that the question of jobs was on everyone's mind. Where would they find work around the district?

It was through the social differences, however, that an unexpected dynamic emerged that was to change the community and create the chance of new cohesion. With a population of only 2,300, Deloraine has just two banks and four pubs yet it has ten churches and six service organisations, including Apex, Rotary, Lions and the women's group, Inner Wheel. This has given the town a strong community base, which with an active council, has seen it win the Tasmanian Tidy Towns award on three occasions—the only town so far to do so.

This community spirit has been an important factor in the town for the past two decades. In a sense, it can be traced to 1981 when the local Rotary Club started the Tasmanian Cottage Industry Exhibition and Craft Fair. As they began organising the fair, it was soon evident that most of the local craftspeople were the hippies out at Jacky's Marsh and Golden Valley. In turn, these creative artisans suddenly found an outlet for their goods at a fair run by people whom they regarded as staid. The Rotarians began to realise that the hippies had something to offer.

The two decades since that original fair have seen the event become not just a major annual Tasmanian attraction, but a national one. From 30 stallholders in its first year, the fair now has more than 200 craftspeople and attracts up to 30,000 people over the four days it is held in November. Profits now annually exceed $100,000, which the Rotary Club donates to community organisations within the Deloraine and surrounding community.

The club was also instrumental in another development when in 1991 the Meander Valley Enterprise Centre was incorporated with the assistance of seed funding from both Rotary and Deloraine Council. The centre offers a range of services to help small business and helps community based organisations with feasibility studies, funding applications, and strategic and business plans likely to provide economic benefits for the Meander Valley area.

Deloraine had always had a strong arts community, with the longest established youth drama festival in the state for example, but the craft fair gave the community the chance to channel the arts focus in a new direction, encouraging a nascent craft community to consolidate around the town.

The town also boasts one of the most remarkable—if not widely known—community achievements in Australia in the form of the 'Yarns' project. 'Yarns' is the story of the Meander Valley told in four large silk panels, each measuring 3.5 by 4 metres and representing the various seasons. It helped Deloraine win the National Australia Day Council's Australian Community of the Year award in 1997.

The patchwork panels tell the district's history and portray its geography, from the mountains to the rivers and the pastures that support rural industries. They also tell the story of different lifestyles. The first three panels were largely the work of women from more established families, while the fourth panel was sewn by 'alternative' women from the valley and Jacky's Marsh.

'Yarns' was the brainchild of retired local farmer Ned Terry, and has played an important role in further bridging the gap between the two sectors of the community. Ned, whose hobbies include flyfishing and searching for evidence that the Tasmanian Tiger is not extinct, knew the wealth of craft skills and cultural heritage in the Meander Valley. He saw the project as a way to bring the community together. 'Nearly every family had something to do with it,' Ned recalls. 'There were greens, anti-greens, loggers, anti-loggers and they got together to contribute. They all came out of the mountains, there were some very talented people. The "Yarns" committee was even asked for morning tea at Jacky's Marsh—that was a tremendous breakthrough.'

Jeweller Mary Phillips-McLachlan, who runs a studio outside Deloraine, believes the 'Yarns' project helped overcome suspicions on both sides of the community. 'The green issue was very divisive around here,' she says. 'It was a battleground. But there is an acceptance now of different types of people and "Yarns" played an important role in that by providing a link.' Indeed, difference is now recognised as an asset instead of a threat, and a necessary ingredient for the region's progress.

Education is also playing a big role in the fostering of diversity in Deloraine. The Meander Primary School, for example, 10 km outside Deloraine, was facing the threat of closure in the late 1980s when numbers dwindled to around 50 students. The community got together and saved the school, turning the emphasis of its curriculum into one that highlighted cultural diversity and the arts.

Under the guidance of sandal-wearing principal Graeme Pennicott, Meander Primary has doubled its numbers and become a sought-after school for families from Deloraine and surrounding areas. The school is the community online access centre, with Graeme having vacated his office to provide the people of the village a room where they can access the internet 24 hours a day. 'We are the hub of the community,' he says. 'We are like an extended family.'

The school is heavily involved in the Deloraine Dramatic Society and in 2000, for example, staged *A Midsummer Night's Dream* with pupils from kindergarten to Year 6. 'The arts and music people are all part of the community and they come to the school,' Graeme explains. 'We have an arts afternoon every Wednesday. Traditionally, many people are wary of coming into a classroom, but if you can tap into their strengths they are happier to do so. We have ideas, open it up to the community and bring them in. Even people who are not necessarily family will get involved.' The effect of this on the community is clear to him: 'As more and more things happen there is a spiralling

Graeme Pennicott, principal of Meander Primary School, believes it is critical for communities to develop artistic talents if they are to survive. (Peter Rees)

up rather than down. What happens is that people lift their game.'

Jane Bennett believes the Meander School is a role model for many rural and regional communities in Australia. 'If you look at communities that have developed a can–do attitude and communities that are supporting new initiatives with creative things happening in them, they have several things in common,' she says. 'The most important one is that they have a really vibrant arts culture which encourages entrepreneurship and people to be different. It will support crazy ideas and not just encourage people to think laterally but support and nurture them in what they are doing. In a great many of our rural communities it is definitely lacking.'

To Jane, one of the big handicaps for the bush is the conser-vative attitudes that have been inculcated over generations. This can breed a negativity among local residents that makes it that much harder for someone with enterprise to start up a new business. 'People who start new businesses do not just need the passing traffic but also the locals to patronise their shop. This is a holistic thing, there needs to be unity in a community such as we've been fortunate to develop in Deloraine. It was creative entrepreneurs and a willingness to accept a diversity of people that developed rural and regional Australia. We need to reignite some of that spirit.'

Jane acknowledges that her venture is not a big business. 'It is quite small by anybody's standards, but where new things start up, communities begin to see hope. When a community has hope it can give itself enough momentum to start generating many new things. Often it takes a few alternatives to move in to make it appealing to others.' Jane's success has prompted other cheese companies, such as the big King Island Dairy Company, to begin production of similar English-style cheeses.

Rather than being daunted by economic and social change, and the often exaggerated physical and psychological barrier of Bass Strait, Deloraine has faced up to the challenges and managed to create a fusion between quite disparate groups—people such as hippies and townspeople, loggers and anti-loggers.

In the process, the area has been reinvigorated and has spawned new leaders—not least being Jane Bennett, whose message is that if people believe in themselves and have the confidence to challenge the status quo with new and different ideas and products then communities can survive.

Meanwhile, don't be surprised if you run across people in Deloraine who can relate personal local encounters with the Tasmanian Tiger. But that's another story of survival . . .

Luck of
the Irish

PORT FAIRY

Jamie McKew had a plot to hatch and the Bush Inn in Geelong seemed
an appropriate place to test it out over a beer or two. He, and the small
group who joined him that night, had not long restarted the Geelong
Folk Music Club. It was August 1977 and, after attending a national
folk festival in Adelaide, Jamie thought they should hold their own
festival. Enthusiasm was high and there was just enough money and
blind faith to give it a go, thanks to successful club nights and
'Bullockies' Balls' bush dances. The question was where? Jamie, a young
resident doctor at Geelong Hospital, suggested a town he knew well—
Port Fairy. It had good venues and amenities and offered a traditional
and historic atmosphere that could be ideal for folk music.

A three-hour drive from Melbourne, Port Fairy is a picturesque fishing
village on Victoria's spectacular 'shipwreck coast'—so named because of
the numerous ships that foundered on the jagged rocks after being
swept ashore by wild Bass Strait storms. According to local history,
Captain James Wishart named the port after his cutter *The Fairy* in the
early nineteenth century, becoming Victoria's first port. A whaling

industry was established. During the 1840s Irish settlers began migrating to the area, attracted by the rich soil for growing potatoes and the good fishing off the coast. Although the town became known as Belfast, the port retained its original name. In 1887 it was officially decided to name the town itself Port Fairy.

Born in 1948, Jamie McKew spent his childhood on a wheat farm at St Arnaud in the Victorian Wimmera. His grandparents lived in Port Fairy, where they had been curators of the town's public gardens. 'Each summer our growing family went to holiday with the grandparents at Port Fairy and one way or another I got to know the town and the people quite well,' he recalls.

The sound of the fiddle and Irish songs were part of Jamie's childhood. His grandparents belonged to a folk music tradition that went back to the early settlers. Whenever he visited them the chords of folk melodies filled the air. His grandmother played the fiddle and his grandfather the banjo. With such a heritage it was natural that he would learn to play banjo as well as the guitar.

With Jamie that night at the Bush Inn were four fellow folkies including his mate Cliff Gilbert-Purssey from Melbourne. They decided to put their plans to the mayor of Port Fairy. Jamie and Cliff drove to the town for the meeting and to inspect facilities. Cliff had fond memories of the area from childhood, of balmy days along the coast, staying with friends at Koroit and exploring Tower Hill, the imposing dormant volcano that is a Port Fairy landmark and known among the local Indigenous people as Tarerer.

He recalls that as he and Jamie drove to Port Fairy, they passed by places with Irish names like Killarney and the Moyne River, where Port Fairy is located. The atmosphere, the colonial architecture, the fishing port, the cosy cottages with open fires, the pubs, and the sheer Irishness of the place lent itself to folk music and dancing revelry. 'There was a bit of magic about it all,' Cliff says. 'Jamie had a grandmother living nearby—a sparkling, energetic woman of 84 who was very much in tune with her garden and people and the world and was just a little bit "fey". A leprechaun would not have been out of place here.' Jamie inherited his grandmother's energy—and maybe even a touch of spritely leprechaun character that would keep him in good stead over the years.

It soon became clear that the township was ideally suited to hold a small music festival as it offered halls, a community centre, old pubs, wonderful camping at the Gardens Caravan Park, and generally a traditional atmosphere. With its colonial seaport history and the beautiful coastal backdrop it had the right feel. 'We knew we had found the place to stage the festival once we were shown around,' Jamie recalls. 'It was the most Celtic–Irish little town in the country.'

The first Port Fairy Folk Festival was held in December 1977. Cliff remembers that while it was just a small festival attended by a few hundred people, it nonetheless all came together. There was a happy and friendly buzz around town. Those locals who were sceptical were won over and those who had backed the idea were pleased and vindicated. A successful relationship had begun.

A second and third festival followed, both successful despite the often unsettled December weather. Camping can be unpleasant at that time of year as it rains and the wind knocks down tent poles. Jamie suggested that the festival should be re-scheduled for the Moomba long weekend in March when the weather is much kinder. 'Once we switched to the March dates in 1980 we had a good run, in fact it has been a dream run with success building upon success,' he says.

As co-founder, Jamie has been closely associated with the festival since its inception, both as an organiser and a performer. He remains director while still working part-time as a doctor. He recalls that in 1978 he played in the Buckleys Bush Band at the Friday night dance in the Drill Hall. 'I remember a few tense moments at the door when some local youths felt that we were on their territory and were not welcome but they couldn't resist the dancing and fun and were soon won over.'

The event has grown to the point where it is recognised as one of the top ten folk festivals internationally. The emphasis of the first festival was on 'Australian Traditional' music but over time the event became more embracing as many international acts in folk, country, blues, jazz, bluegrass, acoustic rock and world roots music appeared. 'There is no shortage of overseas artists who want to come and do the festival,' Jamie says.

Organising a festival in a small town is not without its problems and it took a few years to get on top of the logistics involved in launching an annual event. In 1992 the festival organising body was transferred from the Geelong Folk Music Club to a Port Fairy-based committee. It proved to be an important change.

There was a need to open up more facilities around the town and to get the council behind the festival. In the early days, the stages evolved from the band rotunda, to one truck tray, to one transport, to two transports with covers. Make-do stages were built on beds of 44-gallon drums, leading to some memorable situations. On one occasion in the early '80s Cathal MacConnell of the Scottish group, Boys of the Lough, had to be lifted from the stage still sitting in his chair. He had been pulled out of the Stump Hotel just before the concert and while he is said to have played brilliantly he wasn't up to navigating himself off the high, unstable platform. It was time to build better stages.

Since 1977, more than 2,000 acts and 8,000 artists have appeared at this festival, which transforms the village in a spirit of cultural celebration. Jamie says there have been many highlights for him over the years. They include a 'sensational acoustic–electric concert' by The Bushwackers in 1980; 'the spine-tingling midnight Boys of the Lough concert to open the festival in 1983; the singing of another Scot, Jean Redpath; and the audacity of the band Sirocco leading a hall full of audience out into the street'. But he does not forget the fans who attend—'the wonderful people and great friends we have made'.

Each year bookings are made, programs finalised, marquees are set up on the town's common and between 60,000 and 70,000 people descend to enjoy the festival's four days and three nights. They are drawn not just by the top-line musical acts, but by dance, workshops, street performances, theatre, busking, craft fairs, a children's folk circus and a street festival as well as all the local tourist attractions. Venues are used throughout the town but most of the 300 performances happen in the main festival arena. For many people the festival is an annual ritual that has become bigger and better over the past quarter of a century.

Each year a growing audience that is eager to be part of the event snaps up all 10,000 four-day tickets within days of release. Festival Chairman Bruce Leishman says that every festival has become a wonderful example of the community working together. People are inspired by the challenge of the huge event and also by the spirit of music and fun. 'We are able to support important community projects while contributing to the world of music on an international stage,' he says.

The festival won first prize at the Victorian Tourism Awards in 1993, 1994 and 1995 in the special events category and also won the Australian Tourism Awards in the same years. Surveys show that it has a strong impact on visitors, with nine in ten people saying they plan to return to a future Port Fairy folk festival.

The festival is directly responsible for a massive input into the town's economy of around $2 million each year. Reg Harry, who runs a gift store in Port Fairy, says the momentum of the festival lingers year round, providing an anchor for the region's growing tourist industry. Penny Adamson, who with her husband Nick is proprietor of one of the town's many bed and breakfast establishments, runs the My Port Fairy web page, which keeps visitors informed of what's happening in the town for the festival and beyond.

Even on wet winter weekends Port Fairy hums, helped by the influx of visitors drawn by information on the web page. Penny recognises that the internet is a crucial tool for Port Fairy to promote its reputation as a festival town—it hosts seven festivals during the year. 'The web site's a tempter, the real thing's a delight,' she says.

The festival calendar begins on New Year's Eve with the Moyneyana Festival, which features a big parade and street festival that draws up to 20,000 holidaymakers and runs to the Australia Day long weekend. In February there is the Tarerer 'Back to the Land' Festival, an event that has endeavoured to bring awareness and understanding of local Indigenous culture and to provide a role model for reconciliation. Leading Indigenous artists attend.

The year's highlight is the folk festival in March, followed by the Easter Book Fair in April. The Irish Festival in nearby Koroit is held at the end of April to celebrate the strong Irish influence in the area. Port Fairy marks the start of winter with Rhapsody in June, a festival dedicated to showcasing the talents of Port Fairy and district residents and includes fine food, exhibitions, concerts, history walks, markets, pub music and sporting events. October sees the Spring Music Festival, an event which began in 1989 and is a celebration of Australian and international cultures, drawing up to 6,000 people.

While the festivals have transformed Port Fairy, the town nonetheless still has its characters from yesteryear, such as Bill Digby, a member of a local pioneering family. The family farmed the area for decades before selling parts of its land as the town expanded. Now in his nineties, Bill recalls an incident downtown at the Stump Hotel. He had boycotted the hotel for years and eyebrows were raised when he made a surprise return in 1999. Asked when he had last had a drink there, he replied, 'It was more than 50 years back, in 1948. I was caught here drinking after hours as there was six o'clock closing then. I was escorted from the premises by the local constabulary and fined two pounds to boot'.

It took Bill 51 years to recover from the indignity of having been caught breaking the absurd 'six o'clock swill' laws that were then current. For one reason or another, memories clearly linger in Port Fairy.

With its festival successes, Port Fairy provides a strong reminder of how a positive idea, with motivated people, can turn around the fortunes of a sleepy coastal town. Local leadership and unity of purpose can never be under-estimated.

The Sultan of Sandalwood

STEVE BIRKBECK

Surreal is how Steve Birkbeck feels as he takes off his jeans and sneakers to don a silk suit for a trip to New York or Paris. He would rather be back on the farm or, at least, padding about his sandalwood factory in Albany, on the south coast of Western Australia. But overseas trips to the citadels of fashion and finance have become necessary for the head of the exotically named company, Mt Romance Australia Pty Ltd. It's been quite a journey from the days when he used to carve and sell emu eggs with desert Aborigines.

A brush with bankruptcy threatened to derail his business in 1997, but just five years later Steve has a projected gross annual income of $7 million, a burgeoning biotech involvement in alternative medicine and a range of skin and body care products derived from sandalwood and marketed worldwide under his Santalia label. Along the way, he processed enough sandalwood

Steve Birkbeck ready to negotiate with the great perfume houses of the world. (Courtesy Steve Birkbeck)

to hold the world's largest cellar of matured sandalwood oil and established an industry that has grown from employing six people in 1996 to fifty people now.

The sweet smell of sandalwood permeates the factory. Visitors suddenly find themselves in an exotic environment. 'It's like a Hindu temple,' Steve says. Each week about 10 tonnes of sandalwood comes into the factory, pre-crushed and packed in half-tonne bags. Demand is so strong that Mt Romance has forward sold all its stock of sandalwood powder for ten years, underwriting the growing demand for oil. Shipments of pure Australian sandalwood oil to the French perfume industry have begun. 'We have a productive capacity of $10 million a year of sandalwood oil,' Steve says. 'We've got a lot of cogs moving.'

Behind this success are tenacity, creativity and lateral thinking, but Steve was also ready to take a risk and to not take himself too seriously. He was prepared to accept failure if it came. 'I'm enjoying the journey and I don't see an end destination at a personal level,' he says. 'I'm a risk taker. But at the end of the day I'm a farmer.'

Now in his early forties, Steve exudes a serenity fashioned by adversity in the bush. Stock and athletic, he's confronted drunks and bureaucrats over the years and, despite setbacks, always pushed on, drawn along by determination to achieve a goal that frequently was unclear. The long, straggly brown hair of his youth is still there but the hairline has begun to recede. What has not changed is his preference for black clothes and cars. His personality though is anything but sombre, and reflected in the business acumen he has honed along the way to becoming one of the West's undoubted success stories.

Steve is confident that the company is well on track to become a world leader in essential oils extraction. 'We're the only people in the world with Australian sandalwood oil. In fact, we're now the largest producer and processor of sandalwood and sandalwood oil in the world. Rather than have to go out there and knock on doors, people are knocking on ours.'

That's because companies like Christian Dior and other perfume makers need sandalwood oil. 'There's no replacement of this stuff for them,' he says. 'When you look at sandalwood globally it is a $200 million a year industry. Southern India and East and West Timor have been the sole sources of supply over the past 30 years. In India 250 policemen have been murdered by smugglers in the past five years—defending the last remaining endangered plantations in that country.'

The history of sandalwood can be traced back thousands of

years. Many ancient cultures prized it highly for its aromatic, therapeutic and mystical properties. Indeed, the yellow oil is an elixir as old as civilisation. Pharaohs bathed in it, Tibetan monks meditated with it, and Aboriginal people applied it as a healing salve. It has documented natural analgesic and sedative properties, and is an essential ingredient in the perfumes of many cultures.

Australian sandalwood oil is regarded as having superior anti-inflammatory and anti-microbial compounds that make it an ideal base for cosmetics and body care products. Active fractions in the oil inhibit the growth of harmful bacteria and also soothe and combat skin disorders. Today Australian sandalwood supplies almost half the world demand. On the world market Australian oil fetches around $500 a litre and has been dubbed 'wooden gold'. And right now, Steve's company holds the contract rights to 900 tonnes a year of sandalwood from Western Australia—at present, the only source of the timber on the continent.

Located on the edge of Albany, the Mt Romance sandalwood factory produces both sandalwood and emu oil products. The $15 million company has drawn largely on regional and local expertise and talent. After just four years, in 2001/02 the retail showroom, known as The Sandalwood Factory, was on target to attract 70,000 tourists a year buying more than $1.75 million worth of the company's range of Santalia products. 'We have an industry that the public love, we have a good export story which they like to come and see, so we opened it up to industrial tourism,' Steve says.

Coinciding with the development of the sandalwood oil facility has been the creation of a new fragrance by French master perfumer John La Porte. Introduced to Steve by his

French business associate, La Porte was quick to recognise the potential of Australian sandalwood oil and produced Santalia, a fragrance using sandalwood oil and other compounds including the rare and precious extract Moroccan Rose. One of the company's successful images has been the picture of a young woman staff member who posed for the company's 'Jane' poster. The Jane image is also on postcards and greeting cards, promoting not only Santalia but Albany as a vital, healthy and unspoiled place to live.

Founded in 1826, Albany was a whaling station and the gateway to a premium wool growing and stud breeding area. But more recently, with a population of 25,000, Albany has not had it easy. A severe drought in 2001 coincided with the closure of the Albany Spinning Mill and the Albany Woollen Mill. Both had been in the city for generations and were among the biggest employers in the region. The 2001 collapse of Ansett, the blow to international tourism after the 11 September 2001 terrorist attacks in the US, and the closure of a major department store added to the region's difficulties. 'This has been the hardest and toughest period in a decade,' Steve Birkbeck observes, 'yet within the crisis there are opportunities for growth.'

The growth of Mt Romance as a unique and vibrant niche business is one of the genuine bright spots for Albany. And it could not have happened without emus. In 1981 Steve, then aged 20, became involved in a federally funded emu farm run by the Ngangganawili Aboriginal Community at Wiluna, about halfway between Perth and Alice Springs, on the edge of the Gibson Desert. He was a philosophy student at the University of Western Australia when fate intervened.

A Broome meatworker, father to Steve's best friend, asked them to pick up his treasured 1967 Holden 500 km north of

Perth. They had a few beers before driving back drunk, with Steve at the wheel. He rolled the car but they got out unscathed. The car, however, was a write-off. 'As a point of honour I was indebted to pay back the $500 it was worth,' Steve says. 'I quit uni and landed a job at the Wiluna pub.'

Wiluna was rough, tough and mean, not to mention being located in an extreme desert environment. There were 400 desert tribal Aboriginal people there intermixed with the Warburton mob and Gigalong mob. Spearings and fights were frequent. Venereal disease, rape, sexual abuse and alcoholism were prevalent and even murder was not unknown. On his first shift Steve was punched for refusing to serve beer to someone he thought had already had too much. Bobby Cameron was six feet plus, thickset and knew how to box. His punches hurt.

After six months in Wiluna, Steve left to go back to university. He lasted four weeks before telling his professor he was leaving. The degradation he had witnessed at Wiluna appalled him. 'I was an idealist and I still felt a strong drive that I could actually do something. I certainly wasn't going to do it sitting in a classroom in the city.'

Steve returned to Wiluna. With federal funding, an emu farm had been established in the hope of giving the community an economic base. He started working on the farm and got caught up in the dream. Despite his bad start when he had first arrived in Wiluna, Steve became friends with Bobby Cameron and his brother, Johnny. 'Bobby taught me to carve emu eggs with a Stanley trimmer,' Steve says. After a few months at Wiluna building up a stock of carved eggs, he returned to Perth to market them on behalf of the community. 'Our shells were selling for up to $500 a piece, and more.'

Back in Perth Steve caught up with his petite and pixie-

Emus, as Steve Birkbeck found, can be quite
a handful. (Courtesy Steve Birkbeck)

faced high school sweetheart, Karen. They began living together,
bought a house and embarked on a deep relationship that
continues to this day. But their plans at the time were upended
when the Fraser Government's 'razor gang' slashed funding to
the emu farm. Steve was angered. He has kept a cartoon from
the time showing two bemused emus discussing a man bent
over with his bottom in the air. 'Say, I thought only ostriches
buried their heads in the sand!' the first emu says. 'Obviously,'
says the second, 'this is your first encounter with a federal
minister!' The Wiluna community wanted Steve to return to
run the farm, managing production and marketing.

Steve has always had a flair for marketing, and in 1986 he saw an opportunity with the buildup to the America's Cup, which was held off Fremantle in early 1987. He and Karen organised a fashion parade before an audience of 1,000 people. 'I spent $250,000 making fashion clothes in France and Australia in emu leather,' he says. 'The aim was to sell these clothes for $10,000 each to rich Americans in Fremantle. And we did.'

International interest after the success of the Cup promotion fuelled a $400 million investment in farming emus worldwide. Emu chicks bred at Wiluna were suddenly worth $A380 each. 'We were told in '81 you couldn't tan emu leather,' Steve says. 'We invented the formula for tanning emu leather, built a tannery and then everyone wanted to do it.' These were heady days but the production was more than the market could bear and the emu industry inevitably collapsed. By the time they left Wiluna in 1987 Steve had been sacked three times. Although disillusionment set in, it was with the bureaucratic system and not the people. Over the years he has maintained a strong relationship with Aboriginal elders from Wiluna.

After a few months working in Perth, Steve quit and with Karen bought a 182-hectare cattle farm under the shadow of picturesque Mt Romance on Western Australia's southern coast. They saw themselves living out the rest of their lives on the farm. But they struggled. There was a day that proved a turning point. Karen, pregnant and with their baby on her arm, went to the nearby town of Denmark to cash a cheque to buy food. The bank refused. 'Because of that embarrassment I went back into what I had said to myself I would never do again—farming emus,' Steve says. 'But we moved carefully as we had experience with the emu industry and knew the pitfalls.'

Using emu oil, they began making cosmetics at night after

farming during the day. 'Once the kids were fed and in bed we would put the saucepan and the wooden spoon onto the slow wood combustion stove and warm up our cosmetics. Karen and I would pour them by hand with a jug and I would hand-label on the lounge. We would do that every night until after midnight and then be up the next day. We thrived on it.' Emu oil, they reasoned, had the potential to be developed into a luxury niche market.

Wealthy French investors heard about the emu oil products and travelled to Mt Romance to meet Steve in the old galvanised iron dairy that was now his office. They wanted to invest, initially proposing $250,000 of funding to research the oil's medical properties. They also offered Steve and Karen a trip to France while they considered the deal. If they rejected the proposal they could still have the research results obligation-free. 'I went home that night and we agreed to travel to France. With our three kids still in nappies aged one, two and three,' Steve says. On that trip a partnership was forged and the French invested in Mt Romance with the aim of penetrating the French cosmetics market with emu oil-based products. The partnership prospered with the success of sunscreen sales to skiers on the French Alps. Mt Romance was incorporated in 1993, and in 1996, based on its export success of cosmetics and therapeutics to France, Thailand and Japan, the West Australian Industry Awards recognised the Birkbecks' enterprise as the New Exporter of the Year.

Steve attributes much of Mt Romance's success to the fact that he and Karen, who married in 1984, are complete opposites. 'Karen has an extremely good eye for detail, I don't,' he says. 'I forge forward and Karen comes behind with a broom and sweeps up. Karen is very protective of her own privacy

Karen Birkbeck had to juggle baby daughters and emu chicks along the way from
emu farm in the desert to Mt Romance.
(Courtesy Steve Birkbeck)

whereas I go out and promote and push and take commercial
opportunities. Karen has a good hard eye for saving the cents.
I am not irresponsible—well, maybe a little—but I have no
desire to sit there negotiating over cents. I like to make dollars,
but if you don't have someone saving cents it collapses.'

By 1996 the size of the operation could no longer be contained in the original Mt Romance premises. Karen argued that
they had to move to bigger premises. She had her eye on Albany
as nearby was a state-of-the-art essential oils factory built by the
Indian pharmaceuticals company, Shalaks. The $5 million factory
had opened just two years earlier and was the most advanced
essential oils extraction complex in Australia. But in a foreign

environment the operation was losing money heavily. Steve made an offer for the plant in late 1996.

Shalaks agreed to the sale, on the condition that he pay within a week. Immediate decisions were required if the deal was to proceed. They sold the sunscreen range, which in 1996 had become the third biggest-selling product on the French Alps, while retaining their holdings in Thailand and Japan. They also reconsidered their commitment to their farm at Denmark. 'We sold and moved 100-plus km to the big smoke of Albany, population then 20,000—an isolated country town in this isolated state of ours,' Steve says.

Steve and Karen had not long bought the factory when in October 1996 the Asian financial markets collapsed. Overnight Mt Romance's budgeted turnover for 1996/97 of $2.5 million was more than halved. 'We went into survival mode,' Steve says. 'It was a critical time for us. We looked at our problems with emu and considered alternatives.' Their focus turned to the state's sandalwood resources.

Sandalwood was Western Australia's first export industry, supplying the Chinese joss stick market in the nineteenth century. The first shipment of 4 tons was sent to the Far East in 1845. In 1901, the new state of Western Australia exported almost 8,000 tons of 'wooden gold'. As more land was cleared, more and more sandalwood came onto the market. When civil war broke out in China and the lucrative export market collapsed, mountains of wood stockpiled on the wharves. From the early 1930s the industry was regulated with strict quotas and only licensed cutters harvesting wood from the bush. From 1919 until the 1960s, a West Perth perfume company made native sandalwood oil products. Eventually, supply problems led to the closure of the local extraction industry in 1972. But the Western

Australian Government was still harvesting and exporting the timber.

Steve Birkbeck saw an opportunity. He determined that the problems surrounding sandalwood oil extraction were related to viability. It was a low-yield oil with an insecure supply base. But there was another side to the equation. 'We realised that with the Asian economies in turmoil the Government was experiencing a downturn in exports and a surplus of sandalwood was building up, so we went to the Government with a plan in mind.' This involved Mt Romance extracting oil from the timber with the processed wood then being sold to China. There it could still be turned into incense sticks because just enough oil remained— and the timber would bring the same price as before.

In early discussions with a venture capital fund looking to invest, Steve was advised that he would need to secure a significant percentage of the Western Australian sandalwood supply in order to be considered seriously for funding. Mt Romance tendered for the rights to harvest sandalwood, winning the contract in September 1998 for half of Western Australia's sandalwood production. This meant the company was guaranteed 1,000 tonnes a year over a ten-year period. Shortly after, European pharmaceutical interests invested in the company.

Having attracted multi-million dollar venture capital, Mt Romance developed custom-built technology to process the sandalwood. The transition was a difficult period but throughout it, Steve remained positive that Mt Romance would emerge stronger. 'It was high risk,' he says. 'There was no script. We had to create new extraction technology. In hindsight, we cracked it by 1999.'

Mt Romance oil reached the market in November 1999. Some was sold in Australia and Asia, aimed specifically at the aromatherapy and incense industries, while the remainder was sold to the perfume industry. An important early step towards gaining a toehold in the cutthroat world market of health and body care products came when Mt Romance negotiated a joint venture with the US company, Marietta, the world's largest supplier of hotel personal products. Marietta agreed Mt Romance would have a web address on the bottles. 'In luxury hotels the range is presented as a free gift,' Steve says. 'But it has our web address and our brand.'

This is a key part of Mt Romance's marketing strategy as Steve contends that isolated as Australia is, it is inefficient to try and mainstream through traditional retail sectors. 'You don't have the staff on the ground, you don't have the resources to compete with L'Oreal and Yves St Laurent.' Direct marketing was the answer, with a consumer product strategy built upon high margins, the company's own retailing, and no shops taking half the margin. 'You can't go into every pharmacy in Australia and pick up our product. We make the whole lot and direct market it.'

Mt Romance's gross income rose from $2.5 million in 1999/2000 to $4.5 million in 2000/01, and in 2001/02 was expected to reach $7 million. Growth was expected to increase significantly with the volume of wood processed reaching maximum capacity in 2001/02. With this growth, the Birkbecks' share in what began as a family company has been reduced to 60 per cent. Steve believes there is a critical point reached for companies like Mt Romance. 'At some point in a small company, the fundamental issue in going to the next level is taking away your own ownership. You've got to genuinely delegate and encourage other people and be willing to recognise the effort that others put in. You can get too hooked up in protecting your asset and not be willing to take some risks that keep the growth spurts there.'

In this regard, Mt Romance is expanding into biotechnology and is looking at potential acquisition and merger opportunities within complementary health care. The company has patented a blood pressure aromatherapy delivery system that it hopes to launch under licence in the Australian market. Steve expects commercial opportunities to open up as Mt Romance moves into complementary health, including treatment for anxiety and depression.

'If you look at raw sandalwood you have a $5 million a year export,' he says. 'If you then turn that into sandalwood oil you have around $10 million of exports. If you take that a bit further as we do with a few cosmetics and a few topical therapeutics you have a $50 million product. Realistically, with a little bit more value adding in our research and development, we will take that to $100 million. But if we can develop product applications that can be licensed and their intellectual property protected in relation to hyperventilation, anxiety and breathing disorders—three things that are causative to blood pressure and asthma—then we are talking a $500 million biotech opportunity. All those things are possible with sandalwood.'

Long-term plans include phasing in plantation timber to ensure sustainability of sandalwood as a resource. At present, it is grown in saline areas of Western Australia. Steve encourages farmers in his own state as well as in South Australia, Victoria, New South Wales and Queensland to grow the timber. He argues that property owners could put 5 to 10 per cent of their farm down to sandalwood without having to depend on it as their sole revenue source.

The species is indigenous to South Australia and Western

Australia, but the South Australian stands were overexploited and there are now only small pockets left that are not suitable for commercial extraction. Already, there are around 50 sandalwood plantings in Victoria, New South Wales and Queensland. Sandalwood nuts from Western Australia are being shipped interstate. But all of this takes time and patience. For a perfume producer, it will take between fifteen and 25 years before the trees reach a useful stage of maturity. But it may be possible to harvest after about ten to fifteen years for a pharmaceutical product that is suitable for the reduction of inflammation, for example, of the respiratory tract in asthma, or plaque build-up in arteries.

As Mt Romance expands, Steve has been conscious of a need to repay the Albany community's goodwill. 'The community has played a large part in our financial bread and butter,' he acknowledges. 'Communities deserve a dividend, but generally the downside is a complete removal of that community dividend investment from regional Australia. Multinational, or even Perth and eastern states' companies, mostly take a much broader national or global perspective and the local community misses out.'

Mt Romance spends 5 per cent of its gross revenue in community dividend. It offers 23 scholarships for primary and secondary schools in the region, including for Aboriginal students in grades 7, 10 and 12, and for first-year university. The company also provides more than 40 sporting scholarships and sponsorships. 'Last year we put back into the community around $250,000 including donations and sponsorships, which is a big bite out of a small company like ours and we will keep doing that,' Steve says. As chair of a local committee, he also helped raise $5 million towards a joint venture with the University of Western Australia to open a campus in Albany.

But the holistic philosophy does not end there. A key part of Steve's commitment has involved Mt Romance compiling a list of both orthodox and alternative health infrastructure in the Albany region. The company has conducted meetings with various groups seeking suggestions on where it could properly fund a narrowly defined health project that would be community owned. With more than 30 per cent of 30,000-plus people in the region over the age of 60, compared with the state average of 12 per cent, the feedback not surprisingly has focused on aged care and the health industry. Steve's philosophy involves stimulating others to join Mt Romance in increasing the quality of available preventive health care.

The revival of the sandalwood industry raises comparisons with the dramatic growth in the woodchipping of blue gums that has occurred in Western Australia. But whereas a tonne of woodchipped blue gum is worth about twenty dollars, Mt Romance pays $5,000-plus a tonne for sandalwood—a 2,500 per cent higher gross revenue. In an era when diversification is considered essential throughout rural Australia, Mt Romance has provided the ideal opportunity for farmers to look at establishing high value sandalwood plantations as an alternative source of income.

But Steve warns of the need to be cautious, having seen the emu industry destroyed because of overproduction. 'Most Australian effort is centred upon production, not marketing,' he says. 'Unfortunately, we will never change the stupid mentality that forces us to produce an excess of wool or whatever it happens to be. We need to be regulated as a nation in many agricultural industries. The beauty with sandalwood is that it is precious, it is limited, and we can therefore control its strategic path in the next decade.'

Meanwhile, back on the factory floor at Mt Romance, thousands of visitors continue to stream in to purchase the products and sample the perfume of sandalwood. Since April Fool's Day 2002, a New Age meditation facility called simply 'The Cone' has been evaporating stress levels with sandalwood aroma in a spacious, relaxing, mystical setting complete with stars and cushions. Expect many more Cones soon!

Perhaps it is ironic that the abundance associated with sandalwood essentially comes from a wood that is deemed a parasite. In the bush, sandalwood seedlings have no trouble in tracking down a range of hosts to latch on to. Steve Birkbeck has a vision of fields of frankincense and myrrh acting as host trees to sandalwood through the Australian Outback. It's a vision that resonates with biblical symbolism, suggesting both wealth and potential salvation for many communities.

Reaching for Dreams

LONGREACH

In a cramped radio studio in central western Queensland, Vic Blackwood is living his childhood dream. A couple of blocks away, the Two Mad Hatters—Robin Strang and Kathy Moloney —load up a station wagon full of their goods for the Brisbane Ecka, while overhead a light aircraft emblazoned with the slogan, 'Have Gavel will Travel', proclaims the success of Phil Black's auctioneering business. Welcome to Longreach, 1,184 km north-west of Brisbane, 676 km west of Rockhampton, and location of the Stockman's Hall of Fame, the spiritual home of the Outback.

The stories of Vic Blackwood, the Two Mad Hatters and Phil Black are examples of the resourcefulness of the people of western Queensland. About 4,400 people live in Longreach shire, with 3,800 of these living in the town itself, making it the largest population centre in the region. The surrounding countryside may be flat, dry and dusty as it stretches to the never never, but in Longreach the gardens are manicured, alive with bougainvilleas and palms. Civic pride is evident.

Longreach is a centre of government services for the region, with around 85 per cent of people employed by local, state or federal governments. But while clearly prosperous, the town and the surrounding shire are still recovering from the wool industry's collapse a decade ago. Around this time Vic Blackwood, a big man with a reservoir of energy to match, was living on the New South Wales central coast. He was teaching computing at TAFE and doing part-time radio work on community stations, having honed his skills on Sydney commercial radio filling in on midnight to dawn shifts on the days that nobody wanted to work. The lonely hours of Christmas Day, Boxing Day and New Year's eve graveyard shifts were not much fun. No-one else wanted to do them, however Vic was happy enough to learn the craft of radio patter.

But Vic was restless. He wanted more involvement with radio. The opportunity came when he heard that 4LG in Longreach was on the market. It was a chance to fulfil his life's ambition to run a radio station. 'To be honest, to say it wasn't running terrifically well would be an understatement,' Vic says. After talking it over, Vic and his wife Lesley decided to take the plunge and buy the station. Until then, Vic had never been west of Bathurst. Now he was heading into Queensland's Deep North, unsure of the challenges he faced as he became a refugee from the city. Apart from the matter of picking up a struggling radio station, there was also the problem of coming to grips with a bush culture that was as foreign to him as milking a cow. He faced a huge learning curve: not only did he have to turn the station's performance and profitability around, he had to

Vic Blackwood has made 4LG the voice of the Outback in Queensland. (Peter Rees)

adapt to local traditions, learn regional geography and understand farm terminology.

On the way to Longreach, Lesley told him that if the town was anything like the towns they passed through, 'we won't be staying, we will be going straight back to Sydney'. Fortunately Longreach wasn't. Vic explains that the difference was the attitude of the people. The shopping precinct in the main street had a different feel from many towns. Over the years that has not changed. 'A lot of other towns between Sydney and here are shrinking with empty shops in the main street, whereas here it would be great to be able to find a couple to rent because most, if not all, are fully tenanted all the time,' Vic observes.

'The general atmosphere in the town is that it is going ahead.'
Vic and Lesley made the transition and say now that they have
no interest in returning to the city to live. 'If I go to Sydney I
can't stand it, I can't get back here quickly enough,' Vic says.
'We accept the way of life, we like it.'

From humble beginnings as a stock route junction on the
'long reach' of the Thomson River, which curves lazily past the
town, Longreach developed from the teamsters' stop it once was
beside a large waterhole. The river was discovered by the
explorer Edward Kennedy in 1847, who named it after Sir
Edward Deas Thomson, a notable member of the New South
Wales Legislative Council. The gidgee scrub was explored in
1861 and in 1863, sheep and cattle were overlanded into the
area when the historic Bowen Downs station was established.
By the early 1870s the Mount Cornish outstation had been
established and Longreach developed as a camp for teamsters
who carried supplies to the property. The settlement was officially gazetted as a town in 1887 and land lots were sold the
following year. By 1892 the railway from Barcaldine and the
coast reached the town.

But it was air transport that put Longreach firmly on the
map. Conceived in Cloncurry and born in Winton, Qantas grew
up in Longreach as the success of wool in the 1920s saw the
town boom. The airline was formed in November 1920 and a
booking office was established in Longreach that was soon to
become the centre of their operations. Local graziers funded
the airline and in 1921 a hangar that still stands was built. Given
this central role in the expansion of flight in the bush, Longreach
people were stunned when air services to the town were threatened with the collapse of one regional airline in mid-2001. This
threat only served to remind the town of the need to be ever-

vigilant to protect hard-won benefits.

Now in his fifties, Vic Blackwood recalls that when he arrived a prominent Longreach figure organised a meeting with local business people. One of them was quite vocal after Vic outlined his plans for the radio station to make it a key part of the town again. He got up and said, 'We've heard all this before from people who come out here from the cities. You tell us what you're going to do and you don't do it.' Five years later he told Vic, 'Gee, you're still here and you've actually done most of the things you said you were going to do'. For Vic, this has meant the cost and the inconvenience of commitments that few radio stations would be prepared to undertake. Besides travelling long distances to local shows in surrounding towns through the winter, it also means Vic drives 600 km to call 90 minutes of football on weekends. 'You wouldn't do that anywhere else but out here,' he says.

Radio 4LG's call sign is 'Outback Radio'. The Blackwoods also run a parallel FM station, WestFM, whose call sign is 'Rock in the Outback'. Remarkably, the station is one of just four independently owned radio stations left in Queensland. 'Ours is probably the only one you could call what the Americans describe as "mum and dad radio", whereby the two principals are the sole shareholders . . . myself and my wife, which is a very unusual situation,' Vic says. Lesley leaves the running of the station to Vic and their daughter, Paula, and another three people. 'People who run radio stations in the rest of Australia say it is not possible to run two radio stations 24 hours a day, seven days a week, with five people,' Vic says. The same people work on the AM and FM stations to totally different formats, the FM station aimed at the younger market and the AM at the mature market. 'We have a lot of people with split personalities,' says Vic wryly, admitting to sounding 'about 30 years younger' when he does the FM.

From the outset, Vic's goal was to involve more local people in broadcasting. There were more local interviews and emphasis on events in towns in the broadcasting footprint. While based in Longreach, the station's reach is vast, covering towns rich in history. From Tambo in the south to Hughenden in the north-west, it covers towns such as Barcaldine, where the Labor Party was formed, and Winton, where Banjo Paterson wrote the lyrics for 'Waltzing Matilda'. Effectively, the station covers an area probably twice the size of Victoria, albeit with a sparse listening audience which maybe amounts to 16,000 local people on a good day. But the growth of tourism in the area means this figure is considerably boosted, with visitors accounting for roughly 300,000 bed nights a year. These figures mean the station achieves considerable penetration—which is why it has become such an influential voice in the area with only the ABC as opposition.

Nonetheless, the radio industry's major stations wonder how 4LG survives. There are two things Vic does that makes the station unique. Firstly, with seventeen computers it is completely computerised. Everything has a system and there is no function in the place that is not organised without computer control or assistance. This reduces overheads. Vic believes while it is not the most modern system in the world, it is perhaps the best connected because almost any function can be done from almost any PC in the building.

But there are risks, which soon became apparent in Longreach. When Vic first arrived the power would go off at least four or five times a week. The sight of him wandering around the station's transmitter at 3 a.m., dodging kangaroos and other animals, was common as he tried to get the transmitter working again. In the past couple of years the station has spent around $100,000 on equipment and it is now much more reliable. Also, the problems caused by power interruptions are fewer now because of a new $1.5 million radial feed from Barcaldine.

In western Queensland, Longreach is synonymous with the prosperity of the wool industry in its halcyon days when it was the region's major commodity. Old-timers still recall the 1950s when wool was worth 'a pound a pound'. While this was the high point, the industry remained strong through to the early 1990s, when the wool reserve price scheme collapsed. Advertising records from 4LG during the 1970s and 1980s underline the wealth of the times. They show that the average business person in town was spending more on their advertising than the people in the same businesses spent in 2001. When wool was strong it meant the shearing and pastoral industries, as well as the processing and transport industries, were buoyant.

Life in the town reflected this prosperity. Whereas now there are only a few left, teams of shearers were then to be found in all the small towns. On Friday nights, many of them would come into Longreach with their pay cheques and party until it was time to go back to work again the next week. The graziers would spend up on their twice-monthly visits to town after receiving their cheques back from the sales. Such lifestyles meant a huge amount of money came into Longreach. All of that stopped when the market contracted and the wool stockpile started in the late 1980s. The impact of the stockpile on the Australian wool industry has been profound. When the reserve price scheme collapsed in 1991, growers were left holding nearly 4.7 million bales of their own wool and a $3 billion debt. Worse still, with the equivalent of a year's supply hanging over the market, woolgrowers were condemned to a decade of prices below break-even. It became an economic and psychological dead weight that would not be lifted from the shoulders of growers, agents, buyers and processors for another decade.

The cash flow that came into towns like Longreach gradually diminished as graziers were left with little alternative but to slash wool production. The need for shearers fell away as graziers, also faced with steepling interest rates, sold up or made the switch to beef. No longer were cattle just a sideline; they soon became the dominant interest. But the local economy took a body blow as the need to restructure became imperative. Fortunately for Longreach, along with cattle the infant tourism industry provided a lifeline to western Queensland's economy. It did not take long before towns along the Matilda Highway could see the benefits coming from tourism.

At the forefront of this was the establishment of the Stockman's Hall of Fame in Longreach in 1988. The Hall of Fame generates a level of tourist activity that has made it an Outback icon. Its genesis traces to 1974 when the late Hugh Sawrey, well-known stockman and Outback artist, enlisted supporters for his dream of a memorial to the explorers, overlanders, pioneers and settlers of remote Australia. To build and outfit the Hall of Fame, they had to raise $12.5 million.

A national competition resulted in the selection of a design featuring a sweeping, curved iron roof, vibrant Outback colours and a cathedral-like timber ceiling. Inside, the story of pioneering men and women is told through a blending of audiovisual technology, a thousand historical photographs, traditional artefacts and reproductions. The chronological placement of the exhibits helps to set out the different eras of the Outback, depicting the arrival of the Aborigines, colonisation by the British, exploration by the Europeans, settlement and establishment of mining and rural industries. The effect of the Hall of Fame has been to give Longreach a national focus that has formed a strong base for tourism, with around one million visitors making the trek to the central west in the fourteen years since the hall's opening.

Surrounding towns took note of its success and it became a catalyst for further growth as each looked at what its history had to offer. The impetus of the Hall of Fame saw Barcaldine establish the Australian Workers Heritage Centre in 1991. Under the shade of an old ghost gum—known as the Tree of Knowledge—shearers met a century earlier in 1891 during their great strike, deciding to pursue their cause through the ballot box, thus leading to the development of the Australian Labor Party.

In 1895, following another shearers' strike, the death of a swagman and the burning of the shearing shed, Banjo Paterson visited Dagworth Station, near Winton. His friend's sister, Christina MacPherson, played a tune for Banjo and the result was 'Waltzing Matilda', Australia's unofficial national anthem. First played at the North Gregory Hotel in 1895, the tune's centenary provided the basis for the development of the Waltzing Matilda Centre, which opened in 1998. Blackall, where legendary shearer Jackie Howe set a world record in 1892 by shearing 321 sheep in seven hours 40 minutes with blade shears, restored its woolscour, which operated from 1908 to 1978. It is believed to be the only complete operation of its kind in Australia with the original steam-driven machinery still in place. In 2002, the cleverly designed Qantas Founder's Museum opened in Longreach, marking the town's important role in the early days of the airline. Underlying Longreach's status as a focal point of the Outback was a decision by Queensland Rail to choose the town as the destination for a one-off visit by the luxury Great South Pacific Express in the Year of the Outback.

Besides the region's history, the unique climate and environment also generate an income source. Many properties now offer farm stays and the Thomson River has become a popular tourism venue with its river cruises, when flows permit, to experience the birdlife and enchanting sunsets. Importantly, the Longreach Shire Council got behind the industry with a decision to spend more than $1 million on upgrading the airport runway, thereby allowing bigger and faster aircraft in to service the region. Barcaldine also has a significant airport to further strengthen the tourism support base. Each of the towns has maintained its own individual character and the interest in promoting tourism has probably changed western Queensland forever.

Through such transition periods it is critical for towns to have councils that are sensitive to the emerging problems and in this sense Longreach has been well-served by the council led by Mayor Joan Moloney. As an airline hostess one night years ago, she was forced to stay overnight in Longreach when the flight was delayed. The delay was serendipitous, for she met her future husband. A grazier, he soon persuaded her to leave Brisbane, move to Longreach, marry and settle down. This softly spoken and diminutive woman has displayed a deft touch in guiding Longreach as it faced up to the challenge of economic change and the need to establish new directions. Indeed, she well knew the problems of the local economy after the collapse of the wool industry as she came from a large local property. Joan was elected to council in 1987 and became mayor in 1994 when the region was in transition from sheep to cattle and the new wave of tourism was still in its infancy.

She notes that as a town, Longreach has diversified—not just through the switch from sheep to cattle and the greater focus on tourism, but also with the growth of government services. Longreach has become an education centre through the expansion of the Pastoral College and the School of Distance Education that serves a vast area—like 4LG's broadcast footprint. It is also a medical service town, with specialists visiting frequently. Longreach is now keeping its residents rather than seeing them leave for jobs in the cities. 'Importantly, people are retiring here rather than going to the coast,' Joan says.

Like Mayor Moloney, Robin Strang experienced the impact of the wool industry's collapse which saw her and her husband, Alan, sell their outlying property and move into Longreach in 1993 and establish a bed and breakfast. Out of this decision a thriving cottage industry has grown. So successful in fact that the bed and breakfast business is now leased out. Robin is a self-confessed mad sewer. With a local show coming up, her friend and fellow sewer Kathy Moloney, who lives on the property of Kanandah, 45 minutes outside Longreach, dared Robin to make more hats than she could. 'I made five, she made six,' Robin, a quick-witted blonde, recalls. The hats were a hit and everyone who saw them encouraged them to make more. Robin and Kathy, a tall brunette related by marriage to Joan Moloney, now market together under the name the Two Mad Hatters, and produce a range of ten hat styles.

The business has just about outgrown the Strangs' home. Hats spill out onto the enclosed verandah of their century-old weatherboard house, the French doors to the main bedroom threatening to give way under the weight of stock overflowing

The two Mad Hatters, Robin Strang (left) and Kathy Moloney (right), exuberant at the success of their business. (Peter Rees)

from the cutting tables and hat racks. Women drive long distances to buy. Events such as the Birdsville Races bring customers who detour via Longreach to choose from a Classic, a Kanandah, a Matilda, a Caddie or a Vogue before heading off for a day at the Outback's most fabled track. Together, Kathy and Robin travel to field days and shows, filling up the station wagon and often a trailer as well.

The success of the business is no accident, for Robin had been developing her skills for many years before she took up Kathy's challenge. 'I was a sewer as a kid,' she says. 'As a thirteen-year-old, my mother said to me, "I've had enough of you".' Robin would ask her to make something and then tell her how to improve it by cutting off fabric here or adding a bit there. Her mother told her to do it herself. 'It was the best thing my mother ever did because I'm not a traditional sewer,' she says. 'I use a pattern very loosely. I'll put hot pink and purple together, for example. But when I first started making hats, people wouldn't buy anything if it wasn't black.' Tastes have changed and the venture has proved to be anything but mad. 'It's steamrolled from that 1995 show to the point where we now have eight people between us to cut and sew,' Robin says.

Mostly they are country girls on properties. Often, it provides them with a much-needed second income, but Kathy Moloney points out that it has a marketing bonus. 'These hats are bush hats that are actually handmade in the bush,' she says. 'We've been offered the chance to have them made elsewhere more cheaply but we would never do it because it would mean losing that genuine connection.' Kathy herself knows what it's like to wear two hats as she also works on the family property.

 A couple of blocks from the Strang house, in the main street of Longreach, is another success story of someone who took the risk of going it alone. Phil Black runs an auctioneering business which many thought would not last when he set up in opposition to the established auction houses after one of them fired him. Like Vic Blackwood, he's a relative newcomer—and also someone who grew up in Sydney. In fact, he's been in Longreach fewer years than Vic, having only arrived in 1996. For Phil, the pull of the Outback was strong. Having finished his HSC on a Friday in 1976, he packed on Saturday and left home on Sunday to start work as a jackaroo on Monday near Dubbo. 'Ever since I was a real young fella I wanted to go on the land,' Phil recalls. 'I had relatives who were—Dad was a minister of religion but Mum came off the land.' As a kid, Phil remembers hearing a Leroy Van Dyke song about an auctioneer. He got out and practised and practised the skills an auctioneer required: 'I have a real passion for the stock and station business.'

The first time he saw Longreach he decided that he wanted to live there. 'I worked for my uncle and we came through here about eighteen months before I moved here,' Phil recalls. 'I had a feeling in my bones I could end up here. Eventually I worked a deal with Dalgety's, came here and thirteen months later got fired. Within 30 days I had opened up on my own. I did it really tough for three years but I always believed I would make it.' Now in his mid-forties, sporting a comfortable paunch and a demeanour that suggests a readiness to do a deal leaning on a sliprail fence at any time of the day, Phil borrowed $30,000 to start his business. Six months later he went to the bank and asked for another $10,000. He conceded to the bank that the figures did not look good but with their help he was determined to make it. The bank refused, and to add insult to injury told him they had made a mistake lending him the original funds. 'I was hurting big time, but I'm still with them,' Phil muses.

As an auctioneer who now does business all over Queensland and the Northern Territory, he sees Longreach as 'a real hub and spoke town' that draws business from a long way away, particularly with cattle sales that have seen it develop as a sales centre. Cattle come from east of Hughenden, from up the Gulf of Carpentaria and from the other side of Alice Springs. Annual sales of cattle have quadrupled in Longreach in five years to 100,000 head.

Both Phil Black and Vic Blackwood have experienced a similar feeling of ease in Longreach. Having suffered from insomnia over the years, Vic used to refrain from going for a walk in the middle of the night in Sydney, but in Longreach if he can't sleep at 3 a.m., rather than keep the house awake, he

Auctioneer Phil Black saw the benefits that Longreach offered as a 'hub and spoke town'. (Peter Rees)

walks to the station for a couple of hours to work, before returning home to sleep. 'It's still completely and utterly safe to do that,' he says. 'We have locked our house on two occasions, including when we went overseas. Other than that it never gets locked. Until I bought a new car eighteen months ago I had never locked my car. It's that type of lifestyle.' As Phil Black puts it, 'You can be very insulated in a city whereas here everyone knows what's going on. There's a more complete feeling of well-being for everyone. Even when I was doing no good I was still as busy. I felt I was a local from the first day.' For Phil, one of the signs of acceptance is to be able to walk down the main street and be acknowledged as 'Blackie'.

Vic Blackwood ventures that there are necessarily graduations on the way to acceptance in towns like Longreach for people like him and Phil Black. He believes that he is now 'an accepted newcomer'. 'I guess fifteen years is probably about the time where they think you've been here a little while. We've become accepted as part of the place—we've worked pretty hard at that too, because in order for our business to survive we need to be part of the entire region.' This is a message that Vic always drives home to new announcers when they arrive from the city.

Longreach would seem an unlikely town for people to live their dream, yet even with the collapse of a traditional industry like wool, it is clear that the gaps that emerge create opportunities for new business ventures for people with enterprise and an involvement with the local community. Vic Blackwood, the Two Mad Hatters and Phil Black would all attest to that. Along with Mayor Joan Moloney, they are all playing a part in the transformation of Longreach and western Queensland.

Sub-contracting

HOLBROOK

Heat shimmers from the hull of the submarine HMAS *Otway*, its long black silhouette sitting low against the skyline—in a park. Looking like a beached whale, the *Otway* lies permanently at anchor in the main street of Holbrook in southern New South Wales. The 90-metre long vessel is a magnet for children and adults alike as they clamber over a recent relic of Australia's naval history. The nearest seawater may be 400 kilometres away, but for Holbrook the *Otway* is a way to keep afloat.

Holbrook—population 1,500—is located on the Hume Highway midway between Sydney and Melbourne. Since the *Otway*'s arrival, the volume of traffic through the town has increased 50 per cent to 9,000 cars a day. Now, according to the shire council, 80 per cent of travellers stop if it's their first visit to the town. During holidays, up to 500 people a day visit the submarine, while on other days there are always at least 150 visitors to the display.

Other towns may build big merinos and bananas, or highlight their bushranging heritage, but only Holbrook has the hull of a submarine.

A century and a half after Holbrook was first settled, the *Otway* is the key to a town that has struggled to survive and find an identity. Four name changes within its first 100 years, and more recently its reputation as the 'town where you get booked for speeding', had all fed into its decline.

One Friday in 1824, the explorers Hume and Hovell passed through the district naming it, not surprisingly, Friday Mount. Twelve years later, perhaps being ten miles from somewhere, the name changed to Ten Mile Creek. Around this time German immigration to Australia began in earnest, including to the eastern Riverina. In 1840 a German settler took over the licence for the Woolpack Inn in what would become the town centre. More Germans settled the area and in 1876 the name Germanton was gazetted.

However, with the outbreak of World War I, strong anti-German sentiment arose. In Germanton, pressure quickly built for a name change. Shire councillors heard of the exploits of an English naval lieutenant, Norman Holbrook, who had commanded the British submarine HMS *B11* into the Dardanelles to sink a Turkish battleship. Awarded the Victoria Cross and the French Legion of Honour in December 1914 for his exploits, he became the first naval VC of the war and the first submariner ever to receive the medal. Germanton councillors believed Holbrook was a fitting new name for the town and it was proclaimed on 11 August 1915.

The town forged close links with the Holbrook family. Norman Holbrook visited in 1956, 1969 and in 1975, a year before his death at the age of 88. A model of the *B11* was placed on permanent display in a park named after him, next to Germanton Park. Alongside the *B11* is another link to submarine history, with an original Mark VIII torpedo commemorating the actions of World War I hero Lieutenant H. Stoker and the crew of the RAN submarine HMAS *AE2*.

The connection between Holbrook and the RAN Submarine

Squadron firmed in 1986 when Holbrook Shire Council gave all submariners freedom of entry. While in Holbrook to finalise arrangements, the Navy's Lieutenant Geoff Piesse recalls being shown a drawing of a decommissioned submarine that was being used overseas as a community centre. The possibility of doing something similar in Holbrook was raised.

Two years later and now a civilian, Geoff returned to Holbrook as the town wrestled with the problem of survival when the Hume Highway eventually bypassed it. 'That's when I seriously thought about the idea of doing something with an Oberon class sub,' Geoff recalls. 'I developed three options for doing it, one of which was to use the above-waterline section, which was ultimately adopted.'

In 1990 the town formed a submarine working party. 'There were a lot of sceptics initially, but there was a hard core of us who believed it could be done,' Geoff says. After *Otway's* decommissioning in December 1994, the Navy presented her fin to Holbrook. The submarine committee raised $30,000 to bring the entire above-water superstructure to Holbrook but its tender was unsuccessful. Instead, it went to a scrap merchant.

In England, Norman Holbrook's widow, Gundula, heard of the plan and donated $100,000, with a neighbour giving a further $10,000, enabling the committee to buy the superstructure from the scrap merchant. According to local businessman Roger Geddes, who chaired the committee, the hull had been earmarked for sale to Japan 'for the production of razor blades'.

The hull was cut into sections and carried by semi-trailer down the Hume Highway from Sydney to Holbrook and reconstructed, partially with fibreglass. Roger Geddes remembers confused truckies conversing over their CB radios as it was transported. 'After it was installed, one truckie reported seeing this apparition coming out of the ground fog,' Roger says. 'He sobered up and drove to Melbourne and back convinced he had taken too many beans.'

Holbrook baker Roy Gabriel recounts that a driver stopped at his shop early one winter's morning looking quite pale. Roy asked him what the matter was and if he had been driving too long. 'Been driving far too long, mate,' the driver said. 'I didn't realise how long until I came into this nice little town of yours and suddenly a submarine coming out of the mist tried to overtake me. Your place was the first place I could pull up.'

In June 1997, Gundula Holbrook unveiled a plaque to open the *Otway* Submariners' Memorial at a ceremony attended by more than 3,000 people. Roy Gabriel says the *Otway* has become a conversation piece. 'It has got people asking about the town, generating a lot more interest off the highway. It's certainly had spin-offs for us business-wise and helped put the town on the map. It's confirmed Holbrook as the submarine town.'

Geoff Piesse, who was to become Holbrook Shire Council General Manager, says the *Otway* achieved recognition for a small rural community. 'People now stop and spend money. It may be only a few dollars but it's bringing money into the main street.'

Nearly 100 years may have elapsed since its renaming, but Holbrook has finally found the way to survive and prosper as a small town.

Cracking the Whip

MICK DENIGAN

Mick Denigan wears a broad leather hat with a band of crocodile teeth around the crown. He didn't buy the band, rather he made it himself for he has quite a bit to do with crocodiles. Enough, in fact, to be afraid of them. 'Yeah, they scare me a fair bit, crocodiles,' he says with a Top End drawl. And that's just as well, because Mick sometimes finds himself staring into the eyes of 4-metre-long reptiles in the waterways of the Northern Territory.

In mid-2001, as he was preparing to shoot crocodiles on a property about 300 km south of Darwin, Mick explained that the owners had told him that for the past 40 years crocodiles had been left to breed there in a network of billabongs. Numbering more than 100, they had become quite game, even running at people as they worked. When someone was chased it was clear the time had come to cull the crocs, and doing the job suited Mick just as much as the owners.

Mick runs a whip and leather goods business at Acacia, about an hour south of Darwin on the track to Alice Springs, and his usual supply of skins was drying up. Apart from a modest general store and service station, there's not much at Acacia. The hamlet was isolated enough to be out of bombing range in World War II, and for decades it was one of those places that seemed as if its view of the world would always be shaped by the draining heat and humidity of the thick jungle that is the habitat of crocodiles, pythons and abundant birdlife. The water buffalo introduced from Asia in the nineteenth century have been largely shot out, but there are still feral pigs. At Acacia, time did a passable imitation of standing still.

The crack of a whip in the early 1990s changed all that. And wielding the plaited leather was Mick, a larger-than-life Territorian with sandy hair, a round face and ruddy complexion. With his thick forearms muscled through countless hours of whip cracking, Mick is as tough as well-seasoned kangaroo rawhide. He has the robust demeanour, drawl and the ready smile that one comes to identify with the frontier of the Northern Territory. With hat and sleeveless shirt, Mick could easily be mistaken as the alter ego of Paul Hogan's Crocodile Dundee.

Coincidentally, as you turn off the highway on the way to Mick's there is a small and poignant memorial for a policeman, shot dead at a roadblock in the late 1990s by the man on whom the Crocodile Dundee character was originally based. He had survived the wild but gone troppo. The story serves to remind that uncertainty is ever present in the hostile Outback of the Territory.

Mick and his wife Shauna ply their trade of whip and belt making, along with other leather products, from an isolated part

Mick Denigan ready to crack and sell his whips in Australia and around the world. (Courtesy Mick's Whips)

of Australia, turning a cottage industry into national and international success. What made the difference was that Mick Denigan grasped an opportunity and has succeeded beyond anything he could have imagined.

Born in Bendigo, Victoria, in 1964, Mick's early years were spent in the Victorian coastal town of Orbost and then in Sydney as his father, a bank manager, moved from post to post. He was ten when the family arrived in Darwin. He has made the Northern Territory his home ever since. After leaving school, Mick pulled beers before heading down the track to the Berrimah Research Station.

He worked as a rouseabout, using electric prodders with cattle. Mick reckons they can be 'quite useful in certain circumstances'. He remembers the sharp noise of the prodder and the electric shock it delivers to the cattle. After a while, he says, you only have to use the noise for it to work. Pavlov might agree.

A sharp noise, by chance, would figure in the next stage of his life. In 1988 Mick signed up for the Northern Territory Government's Bicentennial project, Droving Australia, and attended a camp in the Barkly Tableland.

It was aimed at teaching young people the ways of the old stockmen. 'As soon as I cracked those whips I thought, this is all right,' Mick says. 'Cracking them was like hitting a good golf shot every time. A whole new world opened up, working with cattle, utilising whips and horses. But I was more attracted to the whips than the horses.' Mick's interest lay in how they were made. Having learnt to crack a whip, as soon as the project was over he returned to Darwin and bought some books on whip making.

From that visit to the Barkly Tableland would spring an unlikely business career, one that grew from an ageless image of the Outback. The curl and crack of a long whip in the hand of a stockman sitting astride a stockhorse conjures romantic images from Australia's past that Mick was determined to bring to the contemporary world. Here was a niche market inviting expansion. 'My focus has always been on promoting whip cracking as a sport and its place in Australian culture,' he says. 'Nobody knew anything about whips.'

At the time, Mick had a comfortable job with the Australian Quarantine Service. Whip making was a hobby, albeit full time. But that all changed when he was offered a redundancy in 1992. With Shauna he decided to set up a whip and leather goods business. Mick admits there have been plenty of times when he considered throwing it in. 'If I didn't have a good focus I would have given it up years ago and just been happy with a government job,' he says.

Mick knew he would have to personally promote his product and use the latest marketing techniques to secure sales. He says that his experience working in the hospitality industry at the then Darwin Travelodge Hotel, famous for the car in the swimming pool following Cyclone Tracy, helped with the marketing side. He learnt the art of being up-front but still low-key. 'There's a learning curve in manufacturing, getting the price structure right and finding markets. It's a matter of being a bit of a showman, getting out there on the street, cracking whips and getting people interested. It can be a bit daunting.'

Mick the whip cracker and maker became Mick the entrepreneurial showman. He won a whip cracking exhibition in Darwin in 1994 and, with Shauna, began touring nationally, performing at markets and fairs, from North Queensland to Tasmania, from Byron Bay to Rottnest Island.

During the dry season Mick and Shauna would saddle up the van and roll into Darwin for the weekly Mindle Beach markets. Southern tourists, along with those from overseas visiting Darwin from May to October, became enthusiastic buyers of his goods. Shauna was in charge of sales, and remains so. 'In the early days especially when we would go to a function, I would be cracking the whips and Shauna would run the stall,' Mick says. 'She has probably sold more whips than anyone else in the world.' Shauna concurs: 'That'd be pretty accurate.'

A horticulturalist by training, Shauna had not been outside the Territory before she met Mick. Together they would travel the continent for six months of the year in a slow old 12-metre pantechnicon that once carried horses. 'We used to leave when the markets finished in Darwin at the start of November, and we'd get back six months later, at the beginning of May,' Shauna says. 'The truck didn't have a stereo, power steering or air conditioning, but we modified it inside and still had room to carry a four-wheel-drive. We had a kitchen on one side and a workbench on the other. We used to make whips on the way. People could order special whips, and Michael would sit there and make them.'

Shauna recalls that top speed for the truck was 80 km/h downhill in the ranges going to Tamworth. Travelling from Darwin to Katherine—normally a three-hour drive—took a day and a half. 'It was great fun travelling around to all the rodeos, markets and shows,' she says. 'We met all the shop owners we still supply today. After we got the internet site in 1995 it wasn't as necessary, but we would still go down to the Tamworth Country Music Festival. The travelling went from six-month trips to two-month trips.'

Since 1988, Mick estimates he has personally taught more than 20,000 people how to crack a whip. Countless more have learnt through his videos and books. Having won the Northern Territory whip cracking championship three times, he quickly established a reputation as one of the best. His whips became prized by many of Australia's top stockmen.

As his reputation grew, demand for his whips spread in Australia and overseas. They are owned by the rich and famous, including Prince Philip and radio personality John Laws. Presidents and prime ministers, as well as stockmen and pastoralists from Australia's largest cattle stations, also own his whips. Mick is the founding president of the Northern Territory Whip Crackers' Association, and one of his whips is on permanent

Mick and Shauna Denigan first took their whips to their customers by travelling the continent in a 12-metre pantechnicon. (Courtesy of Mick's Whips)

display in Parliament House in Darwin. A Territory legend, Mick won the Northern Territory Manufacturing Exporter of the Year award in 1998–99.

It has been success achieved against the odds. Even in the late 1990s Mick and Shauna had to improvise as they did not even own a computer. To get the business off the ground they took internet orders for whips in true bush fashion—by hooking up an old telephone to a car battery. 'It sounds a little bit rough,' Mick concedes, 'but if we had started the business three or four years earlier we would have had it much tougher. Everything is pretty lucky in life.'

Rough or not, Mick was on the net, and opening up the world as a market made a big difference in getting the business running profitably. 'We were planning on travelling around

America but the internet got us into the American stock whip market in two to three weeks,' Mick says. 'We talked to the major players. A lot of Americans were coming out to Australia and buying whips dirt cheap and taking them back to America. They could see the work that goes into them, buying them for $100 and flogging them off for $1,000. But that enabled me to sell my whips for $1,000. I was making the money, the manufacturer without the middle man, and bringing in those good export dollars.' Mick Denigan had recognised early the potential of having an internet web site to promote his whips and belts across Australia and around the world.

In the late 1990s the Department of Foreign Affairs and Trade (DFAT) looked for ways to boost the profile and advantage of electronic commerce. The department prepared a report entitled *The New Silk Road*. In the report was a reference to the Mick's Whips' web page, and it became the focal point of the official launch.

Virtually overnight, Mick's profile began to climb. His outback whip and leather factory—a long way from the major silk and trade routes of the world—became the best-known example of a successful 'can do' approach to e-commerce, producing a high value boutique product that had a strong niche market.

His web page had begun attracting attention in such notable cattle breeding centres as Amsterdam, Hamburg and San Francisco. For whatever purpose, there were many orders for Mick's Whips, including from a new nightclub in Townsville. 'They wanted a prop in a pioneer bar so they asked me to make a large whip,' Mick says. 'It was the largest whip I have ever produced. The thong was more than 10 metres and the handle at least 2 metres. It was so bloody big I couldn't fit it into my car, so I lashed it to the roof rack and drove and drove through Townsville to personally deliver it. The whip is now in pride of place in the nightclub, along with some wagon wheels and a couple of large croc heads they bought from us.'

Mick's growing exposure to international markets meant there were many lessons for him to master. In one of his first orders from California he wrote out the invoice at $200, thinking 200 Australian dollars was about right, and back came 200 US dollars—then the equivalent of about A$350. Mick has been careful not to alter this aspect of his operation ever since. 'We've done all the hard work, we've got orders coming out of our ears,' he says. 'The past couple of years we've started to do quite well whereas the first six years, you'd make a profit but it wasn't real flash.'

To find Mick's factory you drive down some dusty roads and past a couple of mango tree plantations to his 8-hectare bush-land block. A gate with two big wagon wheels either side marks the location. A huge overhead water tank provides a landmark that is impossible to miss. Neat and tidy, the iron-roofed loft building is fortress-like in its strength. No matter how many Cyclone Tracys might blow through from Darwin and Palmerston, the Mick's Whips factory should withstand any battering from destructive winds.

Although everything is small in scale, the entire production line in the cutting and plaiting rooms is meticulous. Most of the skins he uses come from crocodile farms in the Territory or Queensland, where the reptiles are hatched from eggs taken from the wild. They are grown to 2 metres in smooth concrete pens before being processed for their meat and skins.

Care has to be taken with the skins. 'Because a hide is expensive you've got to keep it in as good condition as possible,' Mick says. 'You've got to be careful you don't nick them with a sharp knife while skinning them.' When the skins arrive from the crocodile farm, Mick sends them to a local tannery where they are tanned and coloured to his specifications. He then cuts the skins to the sizes that he needs for his products.

Mick uses the time-honoured processes of traditional whip making but has also been innovative. All his whips are carefully weighted and balanced to make the action as smooth as possible. 'I have changed the making of whips quite a bit,' he says. 'With some, I put crocodile skin on the handle. That was new. A lot of people who were making whips were not actually cracking them. I do nice tight keepers whereas a lot of people were doing sloppy keepers and that affects the way it handles.' He has also been innovative with whip cracking techniques, inventing routines such as the strobe light whip crack, the fire whip, the golf swing and the cricket swing. Whip crackers all over Australia now use these in performances.

Whips, Mick says, are useful in more ways than one. 'Whip cracking is a very inexpensive sport. It is an aerobic sport so we don't have any bone crunching tackles or high costs. We start off with one particular whip that can last you up to ten years with simple maintenance. I had an order from Eskimos—not just for working their dogs but also for exercise and keeping themselves warm. I also had a golfer who specifically stated he wanted to buy one of my whips to improve his swing—but sadly it was not the Great White Shark.'

Mick makes a selection of seven whips, ranging in price from $40 for a mini-whip to $350 for a Cattle King Stock Whip. Other leather products that he sells include guitar straps, belts, wallets, earrings, key rings and hat bands. By mid-2001, it was not uncommon for him to be selling more than 60 whips a week, generally worth an average of more than $200 each. Around Christmas time, the American market accounts for nearly 60 per cent of sales. 'They just get on the net and start buying,' Mick says.

Microsoft chief Bill Gates, the world's richest man, is numbered among the Americans who own a Mick's Whip. However, he did not order his over the net; rather, he was personally presented with it during a visit to Australia when he was given the rare honour of formally addressing the Federal Cabinet at a meeting in Melbourne. Prime Minister John Howard agreed that the then Deputy Prime Minister, Tim Fischer, should present Gates with a Mick's Whip to symbolise the fruitful partnership between the world's newest technology and something so identified with the past. Gates was fascinated by the background story and success of the Mick's Whips' web page.

By the time of the Sydney Olympics in September 2000 Mick Denigan was giving regular performances around Australia. He was a fixture at the annual Tamworth Country Music Festival, and even performed in the courtyard of Old Parliament House in Canberra during a lunch break of the Constitutional Convention in February 1999. Mick has displayed his whip cracking on television and at big shopping centres such as Warringah Mall, and performed at Melbourne's Moomba festival.

With this established profile, the Olympic Games opening ceremony team, headed by Ric Birch, came up with the idea of a line of whip crackers and horses spread across the arena, with riders carrying the Australian flag. Mick was among the 40 whip crackers from all around Australia who performed in the opening ceremony, in front of an audience of 100,000 people packed into Stadium Australia and broadcast to several billion people worldwide. 'We were all doing synchronised whip cracking, sort of like Irish dancing but with whips and no Guinness,' Mick remembers. 'It was fantastic. The organisation was extremely professional and that's the type of thing that encourages other people to act in a professional manner and to better themselves and aim high.'

Later during the Games, at the Austrade Business Club facility set up on a twin-hull ferry, Mick was introduced to Richard Alston, the Federal Minister for Communications and Information Technology. A bemused Mick heard Alston exclaim that despite all the stories he had heard about him he had begun to doubt whether he was 'for real'. Such was the unique position that Mick found himself in. Here was a boy from back of beyond who had found a successful niche for his skills and was now enjoying a degree of fame somewhere between myth and reality. Alston wished him good luck with his exports. But in truth, Mick has made his own luck.

Besides his whip cracking and making, he has broadened his market presence with the production of a set of videos and CD-ROMS. These provide examples of whip cracking and are designed to help people learn the art. Mick also has a fanciful and amusing yarn that he has published as a novel called *The Whip Cracker*. It tells the story of a young Territorian who travels Australia and the different circumstances he finds himself in, including a stage performance with a whip in a Kings Cross nightclub. 'It cost me $10,000 to publish but the sales more than made up for this,' Mick says. Part of the strategy was to promote his product range, which was included as a separate catalogue at the end.

Mick also writes songs, the inspiration for which he often

draws from the bushland of his property, with lyrics about issues such as being Australian, achieving against the odds and even finding love over the internet. But Mick would have to admit that as a singer, he makes a good whip cracker.

His property is a sanctuary, where he can ride his quadbike through the countryside, swim in the crystal clear water of the wet season creeks or fish for barramundi. The property has provided another avenue for Mick's entrepreneurial flair, giving him the chance to focus on ecological tourism with a plan to build an eco-tourist lodge.

Behind this move was the Northern Territory Government's decision to rename the wet season the green season—a strategy designed to encourage more tourists in the months between October and March when there is the added difficulty of the odd cyclone. The move has brought some success in spreading tourism more evenly throughout the year.

In any case, Mick reckons life in the wet season is not to be missed. 'I love it,' he says. 'The whole place is alive and wet, everything is growing, creeks flowing. But it can be a bit scary with the electrical storms. We had one tree struck about 50 metres from the main shed and it put 70 kilo chunks of wood through the walls.'

Mick's lodge is being built amid a system of creeks and man-made small lakes. The block is the Territory in miniature: rocky, sparse land at the front that gives way to swamp and creek country before opening out into savannah. Frill-necked lizards and kangaroos and an array of birdlife, including jabirus, king-fishers, kookaburras, bower birds, butcher birds, mistletoe birds and black cockatoos are on the property.

The lodge site sits above projected flood lines, on earth dumped from the construction of the property's 80-metre-long,

25-metre-wide and 7-metre-deep main dam. 'Obviously we have a lot of work ahead to complete the development, but it will be substantial to provide extra capacity as tourism hopefully grows,' Mick says. 'In the meantime, the leather factory is in good shape and the business strong enough for us to employ several part-time workers each day to help make the whips and work on related projects such as downloading the internet each morning and processing local and international orders.'

Nonetheless, Mick is realistic about the obstacles faced by small business. He knows the problems of maintaining supplies of raw materials that are so necessary for his business to meet demand and keep going. 'Like all good projects relating to small business there are ups and downs, including difficulties with the supply of quality crocodile skins for the belts and whips,' he says. 'This could create real difficulties at some stage for me, but I'm hopeful about the future.' Particularly when he can find stations that have a crocodile problem.

As Shauna notes, the starting point for their business was a redundancy: 'If Michael hadn't been offered a redundancy from the government then we probably wouldn't have done any of it.' But there is something about the success of Mick Denigan and his whips that reflects the vitality of Darwin and the Top End.

Darwin has endured bombing in World War II and the devastation of Cyclone Tracy in 1974 to emerge into a modern, vibrant city with possibly more dynamism per square kilometre than any other Australian capital city. It is no longer just a sleepy fishing community and service town with a large airport, but a city that is by far the most Asian orientated and least European capital of Australia. It has a natural tendency to 'think north' and 'think Asia', export and tourism. Trade investment and tourism

Mick and Shauna Denigan on the road. (Courtesy of Mick's Whips)

are healthy as the Territory becomes a direct competitor to Tropical North Queensland.

Mick Denigan is part of the more positive dimension of the Australian idiom 'have a go, mate'. As he puts it, 'If you want to do something, like my need to get crocodiles, it can be done. It's that attitude that rural people in Australia associate with straight away—you know, fencing wire and Araldite will fix anything.' Through hard work, a little flair, an ability to connect with new technology as it unfolded and maybe even a little fencing wire, he has moved with the times and reflected the spirit to be found so often in the Northern Territory.

Perfect Match

McLAREN VALE

When winemaker Hugh Hamilton climbed 3 metres up a ladder onto the roof of his old shed, he was surprised by what he saw. He thought he knew his vineyard as well as his favourite red, but it had taken him the best part of a decade to see it like this, giving a viticultural twist to the old saying about not seeing the wood for the trees. From this vantage point the green vines and rolling hills unfolding across the valley to the coast of St Vincent's Gulf were so entrancing that he knew the landscape had to be shared. It can be surprising at times just how close new horizons are. Ask anybody in McLaren Vale: a grape-growing community for more than 150 years, it is seeing itself afresh. And Hugh's climb that day in 1998 is part of that story.

A fifth generation winemaker with 19 hectares in South Australia's McLaren Vale, Hugh is a member of a family whose involvement in the wine industry can be traced back to 1837 when the Hamilton Ewell Vineyard was planted near Glenelg, now an Adelaide beachside suburb. With this planting the Hamiltons established the fledgling colony's first commercial vineyard. The family have been in McLaren Vale since 1947, with Hugh buying his own vineyard and going it alone in 1990. These days, he is among the district's 60 winemakers and 270 independent grape growers who are responsible for McLaren Vale's fine wine reputation. While the big companies have taken over established brands such as Ryecroft, Ingoldby and Reynella, the vineyards are mostly family-owned and small enough to be considered boutique.

Shiraz is the fuel that drives McLaren Vale, and Hugh Hamilton, lean and tanned with a somewhat craggy face, is among the many makers whose rich, robust reds are highly prized. Until April 2001 Hugh did not do cellar door sales for the simple reason that he did not have a cellar door. It was a shortcoming that he and his wife Pam, both in their fifties, wanted to change as demand for their wines built and people asked to visit the vineyard. And that's why Hugh found himself on the shed roof one morning. 'We realised that we needed a public face,' he says. 'Not a tin shed, for those days are gone. People want an experience when they buy a bottle of wine from a vineyard, something they can take home and talk about.'

The dilemma was where to build, and what to build, for Hugh and Pam wanted a structure that had style. Admitting to a certain 'Scottishness', Hugh wanted to build the new cellar door near the vineyard entrance while Pam argued for the more costly site on top of the gentle ridge that runs through the property. Adelaide architect Max Pritchard looked at the options and asked for a ladder. 'Once we were on top of the old shed, just eleven foot six off the ground, suddenly this vista opened up

Hugh and Pam Hamilton in the Rotunda. (Courtesy Hamilton Wines)

before our eyes,' Hugh recalls. The result is a striking building known as the Rotunda that sits like a peaked hat atop the circular wall of a buried concrete water tank, with ever-changing panoramic views to the Mt Lofty Ranges rising above the neat rows of vine-covered fields.

If it is true that Hugh and Pam Hamilton in particular had their eyes opened, it is also true for McLaren Vale in general. Despite the undoubted quality of its wines, the region has been a late starter not just in recognising what it has to offer but also in promoting itself. For generations McLaren Vale grapes were plundered by big wine companies in other regions and blended as their own, with no acknowledgement of their geographical source. Fabulous wines bearing labels from regions such as the Barossa and Hunter valleys frequently had a good dose of Mc-Laren Vale grapes. The winemakers of McLaren Vale muttered dark thoughts but went on doing what they did best, which was growing grapes. A lack of unity of purpose, and belated recognition that grape growing was better suited to the region and more profitable than the traditional mixed farming, hindered progress.

The valley was originally surveyed in 1839 by a Scotsman, John McLaren, who named it McLaren Vale. Early life was founded on farming, with an emphasis on cereal crops. Grapes were first grown there in 1851 at Hope Farm, which in later years would become the famed Seaview winery. The first half of the twentieth century were not good years for the McLaren Vale wine industry. Although winemaking knowledge and experience grew and the quality of the wine improved, the industry languished. By the end of World War II the McLaren Vale wine region had all but lost its identity and the quality of its wine had been compromised. In the early post-war years the downward trend showed no sign of reversing. Wine continued to be shipped out of the region for bottling in other regions, with only three wineries producing and bottling wine under their own labels. To all intents and purposes, McLaren Vale had little identity as a quality table wine region.

From the mid-1960s, however, the Australian wine industry experienced a renaissance as the lifestyle of Australians underwent enormous change mostly as a result of post-war migration from Europe. Eating and drinking assumed new importance. Australians began to drink less sweet fortified wine, instead turning to drier table wine. A rapid expansion of grape production in the early 1970s followed to meet this change, with traditional sweet wine varieties grubbed out.

Licensing laws were relaxed in the 1960s. People no longer had to ask for a 'strong coffee' if they wanted a brandy in an

Adelaide nightclub. These forces of change meant that McLaren Vale was well-placed for people living in Adelaide who wanted to drive down to buy bulk wine or, in some cases, to establish their own hobby vineyards. Many smaller growers, disappointed by the attitudes of the bigger wine companies, also began to make their own wines. The revival of McLaren Vale was underway.

A factor in the region's history has been its proximity to Adelaide. Although the South Australian capital may be a mere 40 km to the north, McLaren Vale is too far to be a suburb. The closure of the rail service in the 1960s and the lack of a fast road meant that it remained a rural backwater and able to avoid Adelaide's urban sprawl. While a recently opened express-way allows the journey to be completed in around 45 minutes from the airport, McLaren Vale has retained its rustic ambience. And even though the old railway lines have been ripped up, the corridor and some ballast remain, thus keeping open the option for a Puffing Billy-style tourist rail link for travel through the vineyards.

A greenbelt of vineyards surrounds the town of about 2,000 people. Unemployment is low, mainly because of the wine industry. The presence of the industry in the town is immedi-ately apparent, with Tatachilla and Hardys selling wine from cellar doors in the main street. 'We're a contained township,' says Sandra Sharp, a local businesswoman and councillor on the Onkaparinga Shire Council. 'The vineyards have created their own boundaries to the size of the town.' Pam Hamilton, a former teacher, remembers that growing up as a teenager in Adelaide she had 'absolutely no aspiration' to live in McLaren Vale. 'That has changed over the years,' this lively brunette with an ever-present smile, says. 'I have noticed a big change in people's appreciation of this area, mine included.'

That change of appreciation is not least among the wine-makers, who recognised that less irrigation resulted in better grapes. This has seen yields on average drop from eight tonnes per acre to four. In the past decade McLaren Vale winemakers have moved to protect their product from being lost in bottlings and blends from other regions. The introduction of label integrity—the requirement for wine from the original region to be acknowledged regardless of where the final bottling is done—has meant that the reputation of McLaren Vale wines has moved to an even higher level, particularly for shiraz. In the past five years McLaren Vale wineries have consistently won national and international titles for their shirazs. This has lifted both the perception of McLaren Vale and the self-esteem of those producing the wines.

Such success is music to the ears of luminary wine industry figures like d'Arry Osborn and Greg Trott. Both are champions of McLaren Vale, d'Arry having launched his own label, d'Arenberg, on the family's vineyard in 1958, and Greg having bought the rundown Wirra Wirra vineyard in 1969 with his cousin Roger Trott and revitalised it. d'Arry's wines quickly gained cult status among wine drinkers and judges. Iconic wine industry figure Len Evans was an early supporter of d'Arenberg wines, once praising d'Arry for his knowledge and enthusiasm and noting tongue-in-cheek that he was inclined to formality during vintage: 'He wears his old dress shirts as winemaking gear and this is said to give elegance to his reds.' d'Arry was one of the first McLaren Vale winemakers to benefit from the area's revival in the 1960s. Seizing the moment, his legendary 1967 grenache-shiraz blend burgundy-style wine stormed the

The legendary d'Arry Osborn with his son, winemaker Chester. (Courtesy d'Arenberg Wines)

Australian wine show circuit, winning seven trophies and 25 gold medals.

Now in his mid-seventies, d'Arry remains the company's managing director—one, incidentally, who still polishes the floors in the tasting room and adjoining restaurant at 6 a.m. every Monday. A jovial soul, he enjoys few things more than to sit on the restaurant verandah, perched high above McLaren Vale, discussing wines. He recollects first tasting Max Schubert's Penfolds Grange Hermitage: 'Max's first oaky Granges tasted like crushed ants to us, the wine had so much new oak, it was so strange.' Before he began to bottle and sell his own wine, d'Arry recalls a conversation he had with Ben Chaffey, who established the Seaview brand after moving to McLaren Vale in

1949. 'He said that when you looked at statistics Kay Brothers, d'Arenberg and Ingoldby made half the dry red in Australia and we ought to all get together. There was no doubt about it. But Dad wouldn't be in it.'

While McLaren Vale was slow to realise the need to establish marketing structure to promote its wines, there has nonetheless been a long history of cooperation between the vignerons. Greg Trott, the droll-humoured chairman and self-styled 'caretaker' of the ironstone-walled Wirra Wirra cellars, recalls that a few weeks after he acquired the winery in December 1969 he was making wine out in the open. 'When four or five of the local winemakers saw me running around in the middle of the night with a lantern they came and helped me head down tanks and lent any equipment I needed,' he says. 'It was fantastic.' On another occasion Wirra Wirra's crusher broke down and Greg borrowed a replacement from nearby winemaker Jim Ingoldby. Greg brought it back in his ute and crushed grapes through the night. 'Jim came around after a dinner party and helped me crush until four in the morning,' Greg says. 'We had a few more jars, and by that time the pickers were about to arrive and we started all over again.'

Greg says McLaren Vale winemakers started to work together in the late 1960s, as they began to realise the benefits of helping each other to improve the quality of the region's wines. 'Once a year at the end of the vintage we would take all our wines to the one spot and line them all up and spend the morning analysing, identifying where the faults were. It worked tremendously well.' These days there is a wine show instead and the assessment of wines is more formal.

The cooperation continues in different forms. In recent years the McLaren Vale Winemakers Association has erected signposts at the start of the main road into the township that carry the names and banners of most of the region's wineries. In another form, this spirit of cooperation has led to monthly cellar door get togethers. Cellar door staff and others in the food and accommodation sector, including owners of more than 50 bed and breakfasts in the area, attend these functions, which rotate through the various wineries. The idea is to allow the winery to show its latest wines, which are tasted with food from one of the local food outlets.

Greg Trott says the benefit is that people get to know everybody else's wares. 'The result is that if you come in and you aren't keen on what I've got then I would know half a dozen more wines at other cellar doors that were more suitable.' Grinning, he adds candidly, 'We're trying to trap the visitor for an extra half a day'. Regardless, people who start buying at one winery will find that the last one they visit will arrange cartage of all their purchases back to their home. Similarly when it comes to food, winery staff can suggest places that might be suitable for a meal. Greg says the cooperation is unique in the wine industry as many winemakers elsewhere are guarded about their wine. 'Down here that's a fallacy. The winemakers have taken a completely different view. You can ring up half a dozen winemakers, "I've got a bit of a problem, come and help me". And they would.'

Blessed with a climate that is said to be more Mediterranean than the Mediterranean, with the moderating influence of the nearby sea tempering the summer heat and the cold winter, McLaren Vale is one of the safest places in the world to grow not only grapes but a bountiful variety of berries, stone fruits and vegetables. In years past this range included almonds, but the vast acreages the almond groves covered have largely gone, given over to more economically viable grape growing. However, the almonds that are still grown are used as the basis for the simple but exotic dukkah—a nut and spice mix that has become one of the area's signature products. Of Persian origin, dukkah mixes superbly with bread dunked in local olive oil as a pre-dinner nibble. In the past decade a significant industry has developed around the olive trees that grow so prolifically. Many of the vineyards now sell olive oil alongside their wines. The marriage of food and wine thus begins at the cellar door.

Five kilometres from McLaren Vale township is the historic village of Willunga. Both were settled in the late 1830s and Willunga in particular retains its heritage stone buildings and footpaths of slate from the local quarries worked by Cornish slate miners. At the back of an 1850s worker's cottage Russell Jeavons runs a unique restaurant that revolves around wood-fired brick ovens. It is not a commercial kitchen; rather Russell has mastered traditional methods of cooking based on the cycle of the fire, with the different stages of the fire used as the oven cools down—even to using the last of the embers to roast the nuts and seeds to make dukkah.

Open only on Friday and Saturday nights, the restaurant serves mainly slow-cooked gourmet pizzas that feature ingredients and produce from the local area. It is not uncommon for 260 people to pass through on a Friday night, eating meals prepared in just two brick ovens. Families sit under a low-slung verandah, around old kitchen tables and chairs in the main dining area notable for its restored canopied lath and plaster ceiling. The scene is alive with kids rolling around the floor, running around the yard, and writing graffiti on the walls of the galvanised iron shed out the back used as a 'ballroom' for parties and tango evenings. The effect conjures up images of Bruegel's sixteenth century paintings of Flemish peasants feasting.

This is no accident but the result of a vision that emerged while Russell was working as the chef at McLaren Vale's Salopian Inn with another key figure in the development of the region's food culture, Pip Forrester. 'I have a real interest in nature and the nature of things,' Russell says. 'Together Pip and I had an enlightenment, almost, that what we needed was always here, close by. We started to interact very intimately with the environment, first in sourcing our food. It unlocked the whole culture that that included. In that process, a "people thing" matured here for me as well. It is not just about food. It is about interaction with people.'

Now in his mid-forties, square-jawed and soft-eyed, Russell grew up in Lakes Entrance in Victoria and worked on fishing boats, where he developed an interest in cooking. He trained professionally as a cook in Melbourne and worked on ocean-going trawlers. He moved to McLaren Vale and a job as chef at the Salopian Inn in the late 1980s.

Born in Sydney, Pip Forrester lived much of her childhood in France, where she became fascinated with the concept of *terroir* in wine and food from the local district. A Cordon Bleu-trained cook, she was an administrator at Flinders University when McLaren Vale entranced her. In 1988 she bought the run-down building that was the Salopian Inn and opened it as a restaurant. The halfway point between Adelaide and Victor Harbour, the slate-floored and stone-walled inn with surrounding galvanised iron verandahs was built in 1851 to service bullock trains.

Working out what was involved in establishing a local 'dining culture' was a challenge for Pip and Russell. They were aware that communities with a strong recognition reflected the nature of the environment and the people, and how they lived. Russell learnt from Pip that the job of a chef was to get food onto the table in its simplest form and to let the local wine finish it. This is the very basis of French–Italian Mediterranean-style cooking. 'There are many layers of learning and I think that together, Pip and I came home,' Russell says.

The culture of dining out in Australia is relatively new. Only 30 or 40 years ago, it was a once a year event for most people, not once a week as it often is now. What people experience when they go to restaurants fascinates Russell. Restaurants, he says, are generally menu focused. 'The person comes in and sits down and the menu becomes the activity with which people interact. Here you interact very differently with the food. People will be sitting at the counter amid food preparation. Right from the moment people walk in the door it is a quite different experience and amazingly they seem to know what to do. It is like reactivating something in our history.'

'The ballroom' is the venue for many birthday parties, particularly 50ths. 'I guarantee 90 per cent of them [those having a 50th birthday party] had a 21st in a shed,' Russell says. 'It's a family way of doing things.' Russell's aim is to get people together in a convivial atmosphere. In the process, a new element has emerged to accompany the food. When he first opened the restaurant there was little or no music or dancing, but these days the strains of tango, waltzes and even AC/DC waft out of the ballroom and the restaurant hums. 'I was into food, but I realised that the ears are not that different from the mouth,' he says. 'They absorb things the same way. This is one of the few places in Australia where people come to tango socially. A lot of my energy goes into this form of nourishment.'

The driving force behind McLaren Vale's thriving reputation for fine food, Pip Forrester, in front of the Salopian Inn, her highly regarded restaurant. (Peter Rees)

While Pip Forrester's professional commitment is to provide a fine dining experience, she is equally committed to helping McLaren Vale realise what it has to offer. 'Wine–food tourism has a big future here but we just don't have the structures in place to capitalise on it. There's great food and wine, a variety of products and interesting people but we're not coordinating their promotion,' she says.

With her mop of blonde hair, the energetic Pip is one of the driving forces behind a move to establish a McLaren Vale action group, known as 'the forum', that aims to overcome this. In the past, the promotion of the region was mostly left to the local wine industry. But the new forum will bring restaurateurs such as Pip, the local tourism body, shopowners and bed and breakfast proprietors together with the wine industry under the one umbrella to coordinate marketing and promotion. 'The winemakers need to be more accepting and the other bits like me need to accept that the winemakers are the senior partner and not resent that but embrace that,' Pip says. 'To work, it's now got to be done holistically. Everything is here, we're not just locked in.'

The forum's focus will be 'Brand McLaren Vale'. 'Come here for a week and if you are interested in wine and food, you will have a fabulous week,' Pip says. 'This is a personal experience, we are not about busloads of 40 or 50 people at a time. We are about smaller groups and "FITS"—free independent travellers. The wineries are not like the Barossa, catering for three or four busloads at a time. They are built for groups to come in and talk to one of the people behind the counter, who is likely to be a family member.'

Since she has made McLaren Vale her home, Pip has closely watched changes in the wine industry, noting that there have been big strides in quality, improved cellar doors and better staffing. 'When I started a lot of winemakers would have long lunches here,' she says. 'Now that's less often the case because they're overseas working their export markets. They're doing their job better. People are beginning to come back here, whether it's buyers from England, film crews from Chicago or people who just want to do a winery tour. In the space of a decade and a half, we have gone from being quite inward looking to outward looking.'

Greg Trott believes that the cooperative spirit among winemakers has begun to spread into the rest of the community. 'We want to see that rapport expanded to all the sectors that make up McLaren Vale,' he says. An issue that bridles, however, is the move by tourism bureaucrats to promote McLaren Vale as part of the greater Fleurieu Peninsula geographical region. 'It is sheer folly,' Pam Hamilton says. 'It should be the other way around as McLaren Vale is the name that people know.'

If such cooperative goals are to be achieved on a community level, spurs along the way are frequently needed to generate new momentum. In this sense, the opening of the Hamiltons' Rotunda in April 2001 has been an important landmark, having an immediate impact not only on Hugh Hamilton's cellar door sales but also on the locals. 'The moment we opened this place the energy that has come from the district has been quite phenomenal,' Hugh says, noting that it has encouraged several wineries to submit plans to improve their cellar doors. 'It has really got people thinking about this area. People are suddenly realising we need an edge, we need things to happen in this district.' But, adds Pam, the wineries are being careful not to tread on each other's toes. 'They won't copy, they will all try to come up with something different.'

The Coriole winery began doing Sunday lunches. Wirra Wirra started picnics with the French bowls game, petanque, played on the lawns outside the winery, with Greg Trott keeping a watchful eye on the competition over a glass of his sparkling shiraz. And Hugh Hamilton has begun oyster Sundays once a month between April and November, opening more than 150 dozen each time for patrons who wash them down with his wines. 'We get the ones that the restaurant trade don't want because they're too big,' he says, displaying a shell the size of a dinner plate.

But that's not where the search for 'an edge' ends. Emboldened by show successes, several vineyards are trying new grape varieties and different blends. 'I have been concerned about this place being a monoculture of shiraz,' Hugh says. 'I understand why because it does shiraz so well. It grows like a weed in McLaren Vale—like something from the *Day of the Triffids*. While others do well, it is the right grape for here.'

d'Arry Osborn believes the area's unique mixture of generally poor soils—ranging from the sought-after terra rossa to sandy loams over clay and limestone, complete with fossilised shells and crayfish—makes good wine 'when it's all mixed up'. He sees it as ideal for other Rhone-style varieties besides shiraz —the white wine varieties viognier, marsanne and rousanne. But, d'Arry hastens to add, McLaren Vale will not neglect shiraz. 'There is no doubt we are recognised as probably the leading producer of shiraz in the world,' he says.

Other vineyards, including Coriole and Hugh Hamilton, are finding success with the Italian variety sangiovese. Hugh, in fact, has gone one step further. He has planted rootlings of perhaps the rarest wine variety in Australia. Known as saperavi, this ancient grape comes from the former USSR country of Georgia. Working with him on this project is a trained Georgian wine-maker who now lives in Adelaide, Lado Uzunashvili. In the days of the former Soviet Union, the Moscow *nomemklatura* was reputed to have drunk saperavi from Moldova. UK wine critic Oz Clarke, who once favourably compared a bottle of old saperavi with aged Chateau Latour from Bordeaux, noted that while quality control was generally all over the shop in Moldova, with 'the stuff they made for Brezhnev and the people in Moscow they took a bit of care otherwise they'd be shot'. Hugh says the Georgian version of the wine is quite intense, sporting a deep red colour and, unusually, red juice. 'It could be three to four years before we have any idea of what it does,' he says. 'The first lot will be a hatful. Whether it stays as a pristine example or gets blended away we will see. First crops are always an unknown.'

Such experimentation is becoming accepted practice in McLaren Vale as the Australian palate becomes more and more sophisticated. Rather than drinking the same stuff every day, Hugh and his fellow winemakers want Australians to open their minds to the sensory challenge of trying different blends and varieties.

And then there is the food. The search for synergy between wine and food is not new and it is clear that the development of the wine industry in McLaren Vale parallels an Australian dining revolution that is well understood in the area. The glaring absence of a McDonald's or any other fast food chain in the town is testament to the perfect match now being fashioned in a community that is belatedly defining itself.

No Longer
for Sale

PETER AND JUDY
HOWARTH

It's the little things that often give an insight into a man. Peter
Howarth picks up litter on evening strolls around the streets of
his Sydney harbourside apartment. By the time he's finished his
walk, he'll frequently have quite a collection. 'It infuriates me
that people who live on this earth, in their country, throw
rubbish all over the place,' he says. 'I can't stand it, I've just got
to pick it up on the way.'

Both Peter and his wife, Judy, find it hard to walk past something that needs fixing. They believe everything interacts: a
community is a 'whole or nothing at all'. It is in Nundle, tucked
away in the foothills of the Great Dividing Range, in the fertile
Peel Valley, that the Howarths have quietly drawn on their financial capital and combined enthusiasm to put their credo to work.
In doing so, they have helped this community to reverse a

Peter and Judy Howarth, who have turned around the fortunes of Nundle. (Courtesy of Duncan Trousdale)

decline that saw businesses close and the town's future threatened as people drifted to the bigger centres.

Nundle is located in a valley at the end of Fossickers Way, 60 km south of Tamworth and 438 km north of Sydney. In 1851 gold was discovered in nearby Swamp Creek, and such was the richness of the mining that between 1852 and 1856 it was estimated that alluvial gold to the value of $1.7 million was extracted. By the 1860s, Nundle was a thriving community with more than 400 Chinese, 700 Europeans and 54 businesses. Forty years later, Nundle was the centre of a prosperous agricultural and mining community.

Today, it is still prime farming land and renowned as a fossicking site for gold and semi-precious stones such as sapphires, zircon, jasper, prase, rhodonite and green crystal. Until recently, however, Nundle was at risk of becoming a ghost town. By the mid-1990s the population, at around 250 people, was not only less than it was in the 1860s but declining further. The old goldmining works known as Mount Misery, which overlook the village, could not have been more aptly named.

Peter and Judy Howarth are graziers living and working on the historic property of Wombramurra, a few kilometres outside Nundle. In the early 1990s they grew increasingly worried about the 'for sale' signs springing up on shops along Jenkins Street. Nundle was on the verge of seeing its essential services, its jobs and, indeed, its people pack up and leave. When the butcher and baker closed, it was evident that Nundle was losing the struggle to survive. The doctor had slipped from visiting five days a week to one. Then the NRMA withdrew its agency. Nundle had reached a critical point with locals nervously awaiting news of births, deaths and marriages to find out if they could keep the two teachers at the local primary school.

The Howarths had run beef cattle and fine wool merinos on their 6,500-hectare property since the mid-1980s. They were also interested in the plight of small country towns and stimulated by the challenge to see just how hard it would be to turn around the decline of such communities. To them, it was also important for Nundle to succeed not just because they needed workers for their property but also because Nundle was their service centre. If the people in the town failed to cope with the economic pressures slowly crushing their businesses out of existence it would have a direct impact on them and the other graziers in the district.

While mindful of the role that governments can play in helping towns and regions, Peter Howarth acknowledges that public resources are nonetheless limited. Therefore, the driving force had to be from within the town and the community itself. 'For four or five years we'd go into town and what we would find was a loss of confidence and, to some degree, a loss of pride in the little town,' Peter recalls. 'No-one wants to invest in a country town with no growth and there were "For Sale" notices all over Nundle. It had a depressing effect on the whole town. We just had to do something about it and one day I guess we just got angry and bought everything that was for sale!'

The Howarths embarked on a mission to lead the revival of the town. In a larger town the demand on their resources would have been beyond the capacity of two people. It was Nundle's size that allowed them to take on the challenge. When Nundle, like so many country towns in an era of bank rationalisation, was threatened with the loss of its bank, the Howarths rallied locals to open accounts in a bid to save it from closure. People did, although the bank was shifted to a more modest building next door. The Howarths had bought the premises and negotiated a deal with the bank to encourage the decision to remain in the town. It now opens for four hours every Friday. They had also bought the old, 1938 art deco-style bank building. They could see potential in the two-storey chamber and manager's residence and over the next two years converted it into the six-bedroom Jenkins Street Guest House, complete with a three-star dining room.

Peter Howarth explains this purchase as a chain reaction: 'The bloke who owned the motor repair business and a general store next door to the original bank building also owned the Nundle motel and he wouldn't sell one without the other. So we bought both of them.' Down the road, the owners of what is locally referred to as the 'bottom shop'—a grocery, petrol station, newsagency and takeaway food store—saw what the Howarths were doing and suggested they buy their business, which had been for sale for several years, as well.

So they did. '. . . We could see the benefits in making the role of each business more clear-cut by putting the newspapers and grocery business in the "top shop" and the tourist information centre, which had been in the council chambers, in the bottom one,' Peter says. 'Then we bought the old boarded-up general store, which became the Lantern Gallery. We didn't know what we wanted to do with that building when we bought it except we knew we didn't want it to be demolished because it is such a great old building.' One wall of the 1890s slab building records in charcoal and pencil the town's shifting fortunes over the decades—who married who, a shooting, when it snowed, even the wins of local champion racehorse Battle Inn. It provides poignant snapshots of Nundle's history.

Besides the guest house and the local hotel, by the end of 2000 the Howarths were leasing out the bank, the top shop, the bottom shop, the café, the Lantern Gallery and the garage. However, the town suffered a setback in July 2001 when a fire burnt down the top shop, leaving residents without groceries and Friday banking facilities for a period while the Howarths rebuilt and made new arrangements for the lessees. The blaze left both the guest house and the Peel Hotel singed. 'Our aim really is to make businesses sustainable and in time sell all of the properties to the owner/operators,' Peter explains. 'We think that becomes a much healthier situation for the community.'

A visit to Nundle underlines the extent to which the Howarths have been able to help the rebuilding of confidence and stimulate activity. In 1999 a builder moved to the town and erected cabins at the riverside park to provide accommodation for the increasing tourist traffic. The trout, yabbie and lavender farms, which predate the Howarths' efforts, have also benefited

Nick Cummins, chef and manager of Nundle's Jenkins Street Guest House.
(Courtesy of Duncan Trousdale)

from the heightened activity. The spin-offs are starting to happen
for Nundle.

Ron Bishop, owner of the Arc-en-Ciel Trout Farm, set up
his business in Nundle in 1982 and now processes 35,000
rainbow trout a year. 'It was a pretty sleepy hollow,' he says.
'There are a lot more tourists who come here now. What the
Howarths have done is all for the better.' Ron describes Peter
Howarth as straight, and a person who says what he thinks but
listens to other people's ideas. 'We could do with a few more
like him,' he says. Joy Burton, owner of the Nundle Yabbie Farm
which she and her family established in 1996, echoes these senti-
ments. 'In many aspects Peter Howarth has turned the town
around,' she says. 'At weekends and holidays the town is buzzing.
We certainly get more people coming to us as a result of the
greater number of tourists in the town and we have expanded

our horizons with it and put in new sheds and facilities for visitors.'

Nick Cummins, chef and manager of the Jenkins Street Guest House, has been involved with the Howarths' revitalisation of Nundle from the start. Originally from Sydney and now in his early thirties, the laconic Cummins has watched Peter and Judy develop their vision together. 'Both are workaholics,' he says. 'Peter thinks in days, Judy in minutes; Peter loves building, is thorough and organised whereas Judy is emotional and passionate. They may be different but they complement each other and believe in the same thing—that the community's health is integral to the health of their property.'

Although the Howarths are now graziers, they have backgrounds in business that held them in good stead 'to do something for Nundle'. Now in his early sixties, tall and solidly built Peter had spent years in real estate development as head of the major property consulting company, Peter Howarth and Associates. He planned, leased and managed landmark shopping centres in Sydney and Canberra. But his vision developed beyond this as he increasingly began thinking he should put something back into the community. In 1974 he was one of a group of cricket lovers who established a charity organisation, the Primary Club of Australia, the condition of membership being a golden duck (out first ball) in cricket. The club has raised more than $2 million for recreational and sporting facilities for people with disabilities. All members pay a $5 'fine' or donation to the club's charities each time an Australian Test player scores a 'primary'.

Peter also began to look beyond Sydney, where he had spent most of his life. 'I didn't have much to do with the bush when I was growing up,' he explains, 'but I went to school with a lot of country kids and often went to their farms and an aunt's sheep property at Gunnedah during school holidays.' In 1971 he bought a property with 10,000 citrus trees in the Dooralong Valley on the New South Wales central coast. He soon found there was no money in citrus and began breeding cattle as a hobby. People told him he could not breed poll Simmental cattle to match the quality of horned Simmentals, so he experimented with embryo transplanting, eventually leading to good quality poll Simmentals.

'But an old bushie told me you couldn't breed good cattle on the coast because the rain leached out all the minerals in the soil. I started looking around for another property,' Peter says. 'I found the nearest place to Dooralong which had good elevation, good soil and regular rainfall was the Nundle area.' In 1983 Peter bought the Nundle property Wyallia, followed by Wombramurra in 1988 and neighbouring Fernview in 1991. He also bought Warrah Ridge and Rockleigh at Quirindi in 1990 and 1994, and others since then. This range of properties enabled him to spread his risk across different microclimates and provide more adequate feed for livestock during drought. The properties became the practical basis for his embrace of holistic philosophy.

Judy Howarth trained as a nurse at Royal Perth Hospital before taking a job with the Royal Flying Doctor Service. She then moved east, ultimately giving up nursing to run a successful boutique, 'Strap', on Sydney's upper north shore for eighteen years. She and Peter met in Marrakech at a mutual friend's fiftieth birthday party in 1989. They married shortly after and made Wombramurra their main home.

Fundamental in shaping the Howarths' thinking was the philosophy of Allan Savory, a former Zimbabwean wildlife biologist, farmer and politician who co-founded the Center for Holistic Management based in Albuquerque, New Mexico in 1984. The Howarths were intrigued by the revolutionary new approach to decision making that Savory had developed. His holistic management principles encompass everything from industry to agriculture, to communities and government and consider humans, their economies and the environment as inseparable.

They began to understand that a way for the village to become more positive about the future was an extension of the holistic principles they embraced on their farms. The viability of the town and farms such as their own were inevitably inter-linked. 'We were out there on Wombramurra and we began to see that unless the whole village worked, then it really amounted to nothing for the families of the staff that live on Wombra-murra,' Peter says. 'The community is a whole. It gets back to this—if properties are going to survive, they need services and the village to survive. Our kids have got to have somewhere to go to school, they've got to have somewhere to shop, it just has to be that "whole" or the district falls apart.'

At the heart of the holistic approach, Allan Savory explains in a book published in 1999, lies a simple testing process that enables people to make decisions that simultaneously consider economic, social and environmental realities, both short and long term. 'Holistic management,' he writes, 'starts with a holistic goal because it establishes at the outset what people want. Because people always act in their own self-interest it is important that they express what *is* in their own interest. In the same breath, however, they must also express what they will have to produce to sustain what they need and want for themselves and for future generations. When they then test decisions toward *that*, they begin to see that keeping the land vital is in their own self-interest, and that building human relationships, rather than destroying them, is in their own self-interest. Their actions begin to reflect this understanding. Self-interest becomes enlightened self-interest.'[1]

Allan Savory focuses on the failure of what he calls 'conventional decision making' to explain problems faced by nations everywhere: among them global climate change, increased droughts and floods, insect outbreaks, deforestation, noxious weeds and soil erosion, pollution, urban drift, social breakdown, poverty, and rising crime and violence. In Savory's view, the root cause is a failure of government: as much as governments will have to change, they cannot lead a change to holistic decision making. 'By definition,' he contends, 'democratically elected leaders cannot lead, other than in crisis or war, but must always follow the will of the majority. That means the change to holistic decision making has to start at the grass roots.'[2]

Savory has visited the Howarths and stayed with them on Wombramurra, discussing in detail his philosophy and how to change the process of making decisions that affect a person's life, their environment and the community in which they live. The first time he came he stayed for two days in the mid-1990s. He also visited Wombramurra in early 2001. Peter Howarth recalls Savory pointing out during his first visit that while they had a focus on their grazing enterprise it was important that they saw the relationship between the property and Nundle

---

1   Allan Savory with Jody Butterfield, *Holistic Management, A New Framework for Decision Making*, Island Press, Washington DC, 1999, p. 565.

2   ibid, p. 566.

as a whole. There was a heavy dependence on one another. 'It made clearer the relationship between the two and the importance of each to the other,' Peter says. 'It simplified the relationship.'

Savory is also responsible for a change in the farming practices on Wombramurra, and the Howarths now use time control, or cell, grazing. The basis of this is to replicate what animals do in the wild. 'They eat, excrete and move on and go around in a circle,' Peter Howarth says. 'Instead of having lots of little groups of animals grazing, you have one big group in a small paddock for short periods of one to five days, where they have a more powerful impact, and then they move on to the next. It works—we've proved it works. But there's more to Savory's philosophy: he's into "the whole". That is, how our town affects our grazing business, and how that in turn affects our lives and those of the local families. It affects what we want our property to look like.'

An aim of the Howarths is to make grazing work better in Australia. Taking into account the food chain as a whole, they refuse to use non-organic fertilisers or chemicals on their properties. Their approach is being noticed. 'We're now generating good business for the town by virtue of the fact that we've got various beef groups coming to look at what we are doing. We have buses of 50 people turning up and staying overnight in town. That's a good example of holism at work—one thing living off another.'

Judy Howarth sees the philosophy as a healthy approach to life and family. 'If there's one section that falls down none of it really is going to work all that well,' she says. 'It's the community, the whole, the land, the trees, the cattle. It all interacts. We were never ever going to be comfortable just sitting out there on Wombramurra, with the ability to do something else and not do it. We just had to do it.'

Peter and Judy had both been successful in their business careers. But they realised that they had reached a point where, as an American had once told Peter, 'We all have to find our greed level'. 'Well, we felt we've found ours and we're keen to put something back,' he says. Having decided to live in rural Australia, they became interested in the community and the challenges faced by rural Australian communities in general. 'There's an enormous challenge today because of the changes in such things as communications, transportation and technology. Once, we used to have three or four families living on a farm. Today, you don't have other families living on a farm, and that means you don't have kids travelling on the school buses to fill the schools. That means the schools and other services start to close down.'

The revival of Nundle had to include the district as a whole. Peter's son, James, became involved, turning the old shearers' quarters on Wombramurra into a hostel for international backpackers known as the Dag Inn. Soon, an average of about 300 backpackers a week were visiting. That generated jobs. Now, they are also given the chance of learning to be a jackaroo or jillaroo. 'We recognised that we needed to find an industry that was going to work in Nundle to create jobs, which in turn would underwrite the retention of essential services,' Peter says.

After some ambivalence, the older residents, as well as the council, swung behind the Howarths. However, it took time for the Howarths to make the transition from outsiders whose motives were viewed with suspicion to accepted members of the community with support for their plans. For some people, it was difficult to realise that their main motive was not profit. This is not an uncommon view in communities that have remained relatively isolated. Inexorably, the townsfolk become comfortable with a status quo that economic conditions impose. Often, it can take the fresh eye of an outsider to shake a community out of its inertia. Living on the edge of the village, the Howarths could take that broader view.

Mayor William Hoad says he has noticed a gradual change in attitude towards the Howarths. 'There was a bit of criticism in the early stages because some of the locals reckoned Peter Howarth was just looking after himself. But I get the feeling that what he's done around the place, what he's done for the district, he's more accepted now.' Indeed, the Howarths were gratified when one old bloke came up to them and said they had not changed the town at all, despite talk that they would ruin it, but had made it better. 'We've got clean shops and all the rats' nests in the grocery store have gone,' he told them.

Word spread about what was happening in Nundle and more young people began to arrive, and stay. Mostly, they were refugees from city life, such as the concert violinist, the economist and architect. Nick Cummins remembers sitting around a table at the Nundle pub one Saturday afternoon with a group of young locals, eight of whom were university educated. By choice, none were using their degrees. Peter Howarth believes the revitalisation of Nundle may have encouraged such people to move to the town. 'They're people who say, "We've had enough of the traffic, the pollution, the concrete buildings in the city. We want to go and have a relationship with the environment now." They don't necessarily want to earn $1,000 a week if they can be out there involved in conservation, and be in contact with the environment. If they can just earn $400 a week they're happy.'

It has not all been easy, however, trying to generate jobs in Nundle. A council initiative to encourage the development of a forest products industry did not get off the ground, while another plan to entice a poultry producer to the area also failed to eventuate. However, in 2001 the 10,000-hectare pine plantation in the hills above Nundle reached maturity after 30 years of growth and was ready for harvesting. The Hanging Rock State Forest will offer enough timber supply for twenty years and new seedlings are being planted, to replace the felled pines. A new multi-million-dollar sawmill has been established, using the latest technology and equipment, imported from the United States. The mill will employ fifteen people. 'In the next year or two, there will be 40-odd truckloads of timber coming out a day through Nundle,' Mayor Hoad says. 'That'll liven the place up a bit. The mill in Nundle will get about 20,000 tonnes a year of what they take out.'

While the milling will provide jobs, other developments are offering the potential to secure Nundle's future. Although their knowledge of tourism was limited, the Howarths believed the town could turn its relative isolation and colonial past to advantage. They implemented a two-stage plan. The first was to provide the facilities tourists expect, such as accommodation and a variety of places to eat and drink. This has increasingly made Nundle a popular day trip for Tamworth tourists. But the second stage, to provide activities and interests that will encourage people to stay for more than just a day, is proving more difficult.

The Howarths bought a share in a woollen mill that had been relocated to Tamworth, with machinery dating from World War I. In late 2000 it was again relocated to Nundle and opened in November that year with the aim of developing a niche

The woollen mill, the Howarths' most recent project for Nundle. (Courtesy of Duncan Trousdale)

tourism market for designer wool products, featuring garments blending wool with linen, silk or hemp. It is already providing employment for local residents and an alternative to the dole. By mid-2001 tourists were visiting Nundle to see the interesting old equipment in operation. A retail shop is also located in the factory and sales have been brisk, with visitors numbering more than a thousand on some weekends. Consideration is being given to using the mill as a teaching resource and for research and development of new products. Importantly, it involves the 'whole' community, with some 28 contract knitters working from home.

Other drawcards are being tried. A Nundle Noodle Market one weekend during 2000 attracted nearly 3,000 people and 20 stalls, along with Chinese dancers and musicians from Sydney. The success of the event means it is being considered as a fixture on the Nundle calendar. Beyond this, the Howarths have two more projects to bring people into the village and to stay a night or two. One is a long-term plan to turn more than 2,400 hectares of Wombramurra into an earth sanctuary enclosed by a feral exclusion fence. All feral animals would be removed, and threatened and endangered native species reintroduced. The other plan involves an observatory with a 40-inch telescope owned by a Tamworth group keen to erect it on the hills at Wombramurra. The viability of each project is currently being evaluated.

Towards the end of 2000, Nundle was hit by a once in a 100-year banker flood that came during the night, swelling the Peel River which runs through the village. Before many people had got out of bed, the flood had been and gone, wreaking devastation as the waters rapidly spread through low-lying areas. Unlike downriver towns such as Gunnedah, Narrabri and Wee Waa, Nundle did not have the luxury of days to prepare for slowly rising rivers after several days of torrential rain and storms. The bridges told the story of the mayhem. The main town bridge was so weakened that speed and weight limits were put in place, and there was talk of building a new structure. The Oakenville Creek Bridge was badly damaged, and the Bowling Alley Bridge, named after the preferred recreation of American goldminers in the 1850s, looked a forlorn sight, sitting in the middle of Chaffey Dam, 12 km away. The huge poles that had propped up the Pearly Gates Bridge for as many years as anyone could remember ended up down by the caravan park, the bridge destroyed. Hay bales weighing 600 kilograms were picked up and scattered around the flood plain like confetti. For a time, the town was isolated. As Nundle worked to recover from the damage, it was hit by another flood. Just four months later, in March 2001, a once in a 50-year flood destroyed yet another bridge in the nearby headwaters of the Peel.

But there was an upside to the floods. Such was the force of the waters in the first flood that huge boulders were dislodged, sweeping down the riverbed like bowling balls, making a fearful noise as they crashed against each other. When the waters subsided the riverscape had radically changed—uncovering new reserves of alluvial gold and precipitating a mini-goldrush in the village. Workers from the nearby woollen mill were among the many locals who panned successfully for gold in their lunch hours for months afterwards. The chance finding of a nugget, however, will not be the sole saviour of Nundle.

Peter Howarth sees Australia—and towns like Nundle—as the last frontier. But if it is to be successful as a tourist venue it has to be carefully managed. 'You've got to have something that's interesting and stimulating to encourage people to come to your town—and not all are suited to tourism and not all will survive,' he says. 'You've got to recognise that. But you can't just sit there and hope that the wheat cheque is going to come in every year. It gets back to creating jobs. Judy and I can put in some of the ingredients to make the town work, like risk capital and energy and ideas, but in the end, a town like Nundle is more than just two people from Sydney coming up and injecting something. What we do has to be sustainable, because if it's not sustainable after we've moved on then it hasn't worked.'

Right now, tourism is gaining momentum; the population is edging towards 350 and the adversity of floods and fire is failing to dint the town's new-found spirit. Nundle is finally showing signs that it may just find the niche that for so long seemed as far away as the goldrush 150 years ago.

Glass Act

WARBURTON

With the sun high above the Gibson Desert and the mercury surging past 40 degrees Celsius, the red centre of Australia is no place for the unwary. Great Central Road travellers on the way from Perth to Cairns via Uluru who fail to observe the warnings of the need to carry emergency water, two spare tyres, and fuel supplies are living dangerously. The Ngaanyatjarra Aboriginal people of Warburton have long known the harshness of this parched land. Even a young Rupert Murdoch discovered that harshness back in 1957 when he visited Warburton as a reporter. He was so moved by the experience that he frequently discussed it with his son Lachlan and others. Yet out of this barrenness something remarkable is happening.

Warburton lies between the Gibson Desert and the Great Victoria Desert in a valley between the Warburton Ranges and Brown Range. Uluru is 900 kilometres to the north-east and Kalgoorlie 900 to the south-west. Shade cloth and a small garden surrounding the town's swimming pool offer an oasis of rare relief amid low hills and spinifex.

While it is the remotest settlement of any size in Australia, the isolation has meant that the Ngaanyatjarra's culture has remained strong.

With a far-sighted arts program—the Warburton Arts Project—this cultural strength has found expression in distinctive artworks that include paintings, ceramics, baskets, decorations, wooden artefacts and spectacular art glass. The town has established itself as a base in the desert for up to 150 Ngaanyatjarra artists. It has also meant that Warburton is home to a unique multi-purpose facility, the Tjulyuru Cultural and Civic Centre.

For the Ngaanyatjarra, *tjukurrpa* is the cultural expression of the link between people and the land. At Tjulyuru, they are fused. Behind the artworks held in the complex is the story of the Ngaanyatjarra and the way they are utilising their *tjukurrpa* in a contemporary way to ensure the survival of their people.

For four decades until the early 1970s Warburton was run by the United Aboriginal Mission, which was part of the great Australian Inland Mission established by Flynn of the Inland. (The Mission now operates as the very effective Frontier Services of Australia.) The first permanent buildings were erected in 1936, and by 1937 there were 300 people in contact with the mission. Gradually more and more nomadic people came to visit the mission, at first staying periodically and then to live there permanently. By the mid-1960s there were about 500 people at the mission. Cultural Centre chairman and community leader, Livingstone West, whose father used to tell him about the early days of contact, says the government told the missionaries they were 'going among savages'. 'But the people always managed to balance Christianity with tribal customs,' Livingstone says wryly.

These days, Warburton is the regional centre for the Ngaanyatjarra Lands that span 250,000 square kilometres. More than 1,800 people, mainly Aborigines, live in the region. They are part of a social system known as the Western Desert Cultural Bloc. Cultural activities and traditional belief systems are an integral part of life for the Ngaanyatjarra. Nationally and internationally there is increasing interest in their work.

Established in 1990, the initial focus of the Warburton Arts Project was on acrylic painting. Long-time project coordinator Albie Viegas recalls that the first paintings were small and modest works. 'Then more people painted and more people saw the need to document in detail,' she says. 'The paintings became larger. It was like collecting a library of knowledge.' Lush colours and deep lines are the hallmarks of the Ngaanyatjarra art represented in works by artists such as Lalla West, Christine West, Betty West, Pulpuru Davies and Elizabeth Holland. Lalla West's large 1994 painting, *Kungkarrangkalpa Tjukurrpa* (the Seven Sisters story), is one such example. This is her best-known work. The painting traverses thousands of kilometres of country as several separate narratives. As with so many of her fellow artists, in her art Lalla portrays hundreds of locations that feature in great song cycles which are maintained and performed regularly in the Central and Western deserts.

As the collection grew in the mid-1990s, the first coordinator of the project, Gary Proctor, introduced the idea of glass. Albie recalls the first time glass was used: 'We were playing around with it and one of the women remarked that she saw the relief work on the glass as similar to body decoration. The transition to glass seemed like a natural extension of the artists' thick painterly lines into the medium.'

The Ngaanyatjarra art glass is based on shapes and swirls that are made into moulds from which large glass pieces are created in subtle but magnificent colours. In the past few years this is the art that has mainly been sold—and in the process helped establish Warburton's reputation in the art world as one of the few Aboriginal communities to work in glass.

Gary Proctor had a vision for a cultural centre—a place where cherished art could be displayed in a gallery and also stored, where old stories could be told and where artists could undertake new works. Albie Viegas says that as the project progressed, the artists became increasingly determined to keep their paintings and were conscious of the need to use quality material to ensure their work endures. Maintaining Ngaanyatjarra culture is a long-term objective of the project, and has been central to the development of the permanent collection. Few paintings have left the community, with the result that Warburton has the largest collection of Indigenous art in the country under the direct ownership and control of Aboriginal people.

This decision to keep their works came as the price for Aboriginal art soared. The Ngaanyatjarra decided their most important art would not disappear into museums and private collections as had happened to the works of many other Aboriginal communities. Theirs was unique and would stay within the community, protecting their cultural heritage for future generations.

In the early 1990s planning for the Tjulyuru Cultural and Civic Centre began. Architect Tania Dennis of Insideout Architects was engaged as the project gained momentum. Tania lived in Warburton for three years, soaking up the culture and consulting the community about the design. The $2.9 million building was funded from a variety of sources, including community enterprises, local government funding and support from Western Mining and CRA.

Opened in October 2000, it has since won a variety of architectural awards, including the Royal Australian Institute of Architects' Tracy Memorial Award in 2001. Set on a low rise in the landscape not far from the Warburton Roadhouse, the centre also houses the main administration for the Shire of Ngaanyatjarraku.

Architecturally, the sandstone-coloured walls and rippling roof lines seem to grow naturally from the desert landscape, while inside local red sand and creek pebbles form the floors. As well, Tania used locally produced art glass made by the *tjitji* (kids) in joinery items. 'We created places for people to work, sit, paint, make things, perform, listen and just to be alone,' Tania explains.

The centre is a place where people can have an immediate and compelling experience of Ngaanyatjarra culture and society. The most important part of the complex is the gallery, with an exhibition program reflecting the lifestyles of the people and based on the Warburton Arts Collection. The exhibition program is rotated several times a year. The collection comprises more than 400 individual paintings, ceramic and architectural art glass works. Within the gallery only a selection of the art is displayed at any one time. But it means that the Ngaanyatjarra people's works are housed within the country they represent and not in some big city gallery.

Albie Viegas says the gallery is a natural extension of the art. 'If you look at some of the work in there, it is almost as if there is no edge to the canvas, the paintings and the stories themselves; they extend far beyond the edge of the canvas. Some of them have that particularly strong quality of extending into the landscape. It is even more potent when the art is being displayed in its own land which inspired it and gives its meaning.'

Like so many Outback communities, Warburton is not immune from the social problems that lead to substance abuse. On one level, the community is tackling the problem with wardens keeping a close eye on the activities of its young people. The sale of petrol and alcohol is controlled in a bid to eliminate substance abuse. But art is providing another way to confront the problem. Through art, the community is using its past to establish cohesiveness. This is providing a focus for youth and building the foundations to cope with contemporary pressures.

At the centre, there are film and pizza nights, where people can drink coffee at the Kapi Café, and school kids can learn about Ngaanyatjarra ways. Livingstone West says now that people have such a facility as the centre, it makes it easier to translate or represent the ideas of Ngaany-atjarra culture to their own family members. 'Being able to show it to young kids is a really strong educational tool; to be able to show our paintings in our own land is a powerful way of holding our people's culture,' he says.

There is yet another aspect to the cultural centre's establishment. The community, according to Livingstone, recognises that reconciliation and communication with other Australians are the most important issues facing the Ngaanyatjarra people. They see the centre as an important step towards engagement with the wider community.

Based on its success of the past decade, the Warburton Arts Project will continue its initiatives in generating, promoting and maintaining the artistic works of the Ngaanyatjarra people. Through touring exhibitions and the creation of such a unique gallery at Warburton, a national and international profile has been built up for local artists. Art and tourism are linked to Warburton's future, and Livingstone says that while it is important for the community to encourage people to visit and buy some art he wants the attractions of Warburton to go beyond this.

Local economic development in Ngaanyatjarra communities is an emerging factor, and the form that it will take, when and if it is fully developed, will depend on the long-term success of current ventures. Some women have tapped into the profitable bush tucker market, supplying produce such as quandongs and berries to Melbourne, Sydney and eventually, with value adding by other people, overseas.

Ngaanyatjarra culture has existed in this area for many thousands of years and how tourism will affect the local region is an unknown issue. But Tania Dennis is confident that the centre will provide a solid foundation for both tourism development and the maintenance of the culture. 'Due to the isolation and sheer size of the region, tourism development may be a slow process but with the centre as a strong core, tourism activities are developing on their own terms with a powerful local cultural identity,' she says.

An upgrade of the Outback highway to create a new route from the

Western Australian goldfields through Warburton and Alice Springs to central Queensland could make tourism more viable. As well, the sealing of the runway at Warburton airstrip could encourage charter air services and regular passenger flights from both Alice Springs and Perth. 'We want to open this up for the whole world,' Livingstone says. 'We've put it on the internet; we did that so the world can see what's happening in Central Australia. There are magnificent places in the bush around here. People around the world know about Uluru and the Olgas [Kata Tjuta] but we've got Yutjari Gorge and more. Not many people know about it. We can take the tourists there and walk them through it. We want to share the secret of this place.' Through the medium of their art and glass the people of Warburton have found such a way.

Thanks to Rupert Murdoch's visit in 1957, there was a precursor to Warburton being in the spotlight. A controversy unfolded between the News Ltd publisher and a Western Australian parliamentary committee after he disputed its findings that Aborigines in Central Australia were suffering greatly from health and other problems. The young Rupert spent several days travelling hundreds of kilometres across Central Australia before writing in his newspaper, the Adelaide *News*, of his visit to the Warburton Mission. The Ngaanyatjarra, he said, were 'fine people steeped in the knowledge of their proud history and great lovers of their own land'. He described a 'swim to remember' in a waterhole near Warburton after he took refuge from the fierce heat, finding the 'glorious coolness' of the fresh water irresistible.

Rupert was as forthright then as he is now. And so are the Ngaanyatjarra. The love of the land and the proud history that Rupert wrote about are the secrets that Livingstone West and the Warburton community are ready to share.

Arizona, Australia

RICHARD AND JUDI MAKIM

On the horizon, when the grasshoppers come, the sky is black. As they swarm across the country after a wet season, the air is dense with the whirr of wings. The mood is ominous. For a grasshopper plague threatens crops. Yet Richard Makim holds no serious concerns as the cloud of insects sweeps through Arizona Station, a 64,000-hectare cattle property in north-west Queensland, for he sees unique advantages rather than short-term destruction.

At Arizona, long accepted grazing practices are being over-turned and the benefits of doing things differently and thinking holistically are apparent. Arizona is one-third open black soil river flood plains country and two-thirds sandy forest where the soil is marginally phosphorous deficient. The only way to get pasture growth sustainably is through recycling nutrients. To this extent, the grasshoppers are the Makims' allies. To recognise that fact, they had to become holistic graziers.

'Like every other farmer, I was terrified at the first sight of grasshoppers before I started thinking holistically,' Richard, one of the beef industry's leaders in northern Australia, says. 'I thought they would wipe me out. But curiously, they never did. When I looked a little closer at what was happening I realised that they didn't stay out on the open grasslands but would blanket the trees in the forest. So it's not a worry when I see them coming now because they don't only eat the grass the cattle eat; rather, they eat the trees and timber with too much tannin that the cattle can't digest.'

The trees quickly recover from the natural pruning, and underneath the branches the grasshoppers leave a carpet of brown, mouse-like droppings. 'The sweetest grass grows in the drip line of the tree where the nutrients are recycling, not just from the leaves but also from the bugs eating them.' From this experience Richard Makim sees profound lessons for Australian farmers: 'I think the writing is on the wall for the fifties' approach where you just nuke everything with antibiotics and weedicides and spray bugs. That creates more problems than it fixes. When you get into holistics you get very interested in making sure that when you knock something out you don't stuff something else. By making sure there are no grasshoppers eating our pastures what else are we collapsing? You've got to have things in balance. It's like Sydney—too many people and you get an environmental mess; too many chooks, pigs or roos and it's the same. It's got to be in balance.'

Balance is the catchcry at Arizona. The station is home to abundant wildlife. Kites, hawks and wedgetail eagles wheel over-head, plains turkeys scamper into the brush, emus dart across the track and freshwater crocodiles laze on the banks of the Saxby River. A big black feral pig looks on from the other side of the river as Richard scans the banks for stray cattle watering in the late afternoon.

In the distance, smoke from scrub fires around the Gulf of Carpentaria, just a few hours to the north, turns the sky a pallid grey. The Saxby, Norman and Flinders rivers, fed by a myriad of stream channels, drain northward towards the plains and shallow waters of the Gulf. During the wet season from October to March these streams can, in big years, transform the surrounding low, flat arid plains into inland seas, the engorged rivers sometimes overflowing their banks to join each other over tens of kilometres, effectively isolating communities. In other years, they may not run at all; such is the variability of the land that Outback Australians have to live with and manage.

Isolation is a reality of life for the Makims. Arizona is located 160 km north of Julia Creek. The closest large city, Townsville, is about 900 km to the east. Self-reliance is a necessity for survival. As Judi Makim puts it, 'You don't have tremendous resources out here, you have to rely on yourselves and just get in and do it.'

Both Richard and Judi have bush backgrounds. Judi grew up in Moree in northern New South Wales and boarded at school in Sydney. She became an air hostess before going to London to work. Returning to Sydney, she and Richard married in 1973. She acknowledges the differences between them—differences which in fact have formed a strong partnership. 'Richard's a big-picture man, he thinks outside the square all the time,' Judi says. 'I'm the checks and balances, and probably see things more realistically and practically. We don't see things

Richard and Judi Makim, whose holistic approach to grazing has assured success for their property, Arizona. (Peter Rees)

competitively—it's interdependence, not independence. That's why we're probably not a bad team.'

Like Judi, the snowy-haired Richard is now in his early fifties. In the heat and dust of Arizona, he is rarely seen without a colourful bandanna around his neck.

While growing up, he learnt from Aborigines how to use fire for mustering. 'We mustered cattle the way they used to muster animals for hunting,' Richard remembers. 'You go out and make a "cool" fire, burn out a little area, like a mosaic. After the fire new green shoots would appear, bringing together the grazing animals.' The nub of the observation remained with him to be re-activated many years later.

A fourth-generation grazier from west of the Great Dividing Range, he moved with his parents to the station alongside Arizona when he was twelve years old. His older sister had won the property in a Queensland land ballot. When she married a neighbour her parents bought her out. Richard became familiar with Arizona when he mustered cattle for its owners in 1977. He had a good idea of how many cattle grazed the vast property. In 1978, after a four-year slump in cattle prices, Richard and Judi made a successful offer for Arizona. Richard's assessment that there were more cattle on the property than the owners thought turned out to be correct, and helped by an upturn in cattle prices, the Makims' big gamble paid off. In the years that followed they raised seven children on Arizona and built a mud brick homestead to suit their needs.

From the dusty track that winds through the downs, bougainvilleas cascade over an archway that leads to the homestead. Surrounded by a 4-metre-wide verandah providing relief from the unrelenting summer heat, the main house is part of a complex of buildings.

To one side, a big vegetable garden provides produce for the homestead during the winter months. In between the main homestead and amenities block is a sylvan garden that Judi has created, with ferns, exotic flowers, neem and peltoferen trees and native shrubs filtering the tropical sun. With its maturity have come the birds—including, for the lower Gulf, a rare native pheasant coucal that flits among the branches. On the open side of the garden the Makims have laid the foundations for another free-standing wing that will complete the complex. When it is built it will also expand Arizona's accommodation potential to cater for eco-tourism as a possible future direction.

In a state where there is heated debate about clearing land

for grazing sheep and cattle, Richard leaves no doubt about where he stands. 'While graziers under economic pressure think they've got to clear it, we'd be putting some of the timber back in,' he says bluntly. 'Certainly there is no argument for clearing it past 30 per cent. To take out more than that is crazy. It might give you a quick fix and quick production, but you're losing your long-term ability to recycle your nutrients. People who have adopted total system techniques find that if they've got timber rates of at least 20 per cent in their pasture they're getting better production than those with totally cleared pasture.' Richard says that while research is limited, there appears to be fungi at work in timber-based pastures which release plant nutrients more readily than microbe-based open grass pastures.

The Makims first heard about Allan Savory's holistic management centre in the United States in the early 1990s. Richard read Savory's book and later attended a Grazing for Profit course based on his methods, and as he puts it, he got the 'Eureka effect'. Pieces began dropping into place. 'There are things that you have known and taken for granted,' he says. 'That hinders you from making a paradigm shift and moving on to the next link in re-interpreting what you're doing.'

On Arizona, stock are rotationally grazed and the pasture then rested, ensuring that the tussocks are not taken down too low as this kills or shortens the roots and hinders recovery time. 'It's understood in grazing that drought or hard times can be artificially created by overusing or overgrazing country,' Richard says. 'Through poor management, this can even occur while understocking.' He notes that when things are in balance, 'it's amazing how they all fit in and work'. He cites the role of dung beetles in taking animal manure down to the root zone and preventing water run-off and erosion.

An important sign is the birdlife. 'Changing your biodiversity affects the birdlife, and if they start to disappear the bugs will get out of sync. People often don't understand the havoc they're creating by shutting off water. If I said I was going to move cattle and move the 'roos out by turning off the water, there might be numerous other things that will collapse. I need to leave high water for birds where the cats can't get them. I know the hawks are still going to pick them off, but I can't do much about that. The birds are going to have to work that one out.' Already pigeon species are increasing—as are the numbers of the rare Julia Creek dunnart, a marsupial mouse that is thought to feed on arthropods.

Like other local rodents and marsupials, the dunnart probably rests in the maze of underground cavities provided by the region's grass-covered, cracking brown soils. Between 1931 and 1972 only four specimens had been collected near Julia Creek and in the surrounding district. To the Makims the dunnarts are an important part of the ecosystem, all of which needs to be protected.

Richard understands the fine line between over- and under-grazing and acknowledges the advantages that technology has brought to farming, not least things like polythene pipe, electric fencing and computerised mapping. Electric fencing is a critical part of the approach. Not only is it cheaper and quicker to run than traditional barbed wire, it is also less damaging to stock and wildlife, such as kangaroos and emus which duck under it, and provides greater stock security. Richard has fenced off his river and creek country and put cattle in open downs country, bringing water out to them instead of having them walk to the river.

This is the opposite of accepted practice. 'Traditionally when they graze this country for six months of the year, our cattle would water at the river in the morning—live down there all day,' he says. 'They would wait for the heat of the day to pass, have a drink and in the evening graze back out again. They would make pads where they walked in and out, which going down to the side of the river created erosion.' Continuous living creates a dustbowl because of the way the cattle stand around all day. It means that they do not eat much grass beyond 1.5 km from water. Yet graziers like the Makims were influenced by what the experts had assured them was right—that cattle would walk five or six kilometres to water. Nobody, Richard says, sat down to do their homework on the nutrition and what it would take to sustain or grow an animal in the drier months of the year.

The principle of having large numbers of cattle together for short times necessitated Richard laying down polythene pipe to carry bore water. With cattle mostly drinking water over a five- to six-hour period every day, it has meant concentrated demand on supply. 'They all come in and want a drink,' Richard says. 'If they came in and drank slowly over 24 hours it wouldn't be a problem but they all come in and want it now. We've got to be delivering 2.5 litres a second for the stock numbers we want.'

Richard Makim has a different view from many other graziers in northern Australia about the type of cattle best suited to the area. No longer content to just run the traditional Brahman, Droughtmaster and Santa Gertrudis cattle, he is exper-imenting with new breeds and crossing them unconventionally.

In the mid-1980s he and twelve other producers joined forces with the CSIRO to import two African breeds—the Tuli and the Boran. DNA testing showed they were sufficiently un-related to the breeds in use in Australia. This bode well for excellent hybrid vigour. The Tuli, an adapted *Bos taurus*, had lived for more than 2,000 years in the tough African environment, surviving ticks and worms and living with tribes that put them under production pressure.

Similarly the Boran, a straight *Bos indicus*, survived in even tougher environments around Ethiopia. The African tribes wanted regular milk and meat supplies, and the Boran had survived and prospered there 700 years after leaving India. To the Africans, cattle were wealth, and therefore subject to production pressures, unlike the Indian subcontinent where they were sacred.

The Boran and the Tuli are now crossed with other herds on Arizona. 'It's like a smorgasbord, you can go out there and select all sorts of cattle to do all sorts of things,' Richard says. 'What we need is fertility, adaptation and the quickest growing meat quality cattle we can produce in this type of environment. We are using a later maturing animal crossed with an early maturing animal to produce a composite bull to be used in a three-way rotation.' There are now six breeds on Arizona, including the Italian Piedmontese, the French Charolais, the British Angus and the *Bos indicus* Brahman.

The goal is smaller females to provide lower maintenance cattle. 'Most of the world is chasing bigger and bigger because bigger is better,' Richard says. 'But bigger is fraught with all sorts of difficulties. You've got higher maintenance cattle needing more grass and you've got calving problems in heifers because bigger cattle have bigger calves. We'd rather the faster growing, early maturing cattle that are slightly smaller in size. Practically everything we're doing comes back to a balancing act of chasing production with fertility and getting maximum numbers of live calves on the ground.'

On Arizona, pasture management drives the system. 'You've got to worry about the grass rather than the cattle,' Richard says. 'If I can cycle carbon better, the perennial grasses are thicker.' And he adds: 'The stock are not the problem. Without education or understanding and applied management, I am the problem. It has been human nature to take what's easy but the system collapses because the balance is upset.'

It is only in the past decade or so that local graziers like the Makims have been trying to 'relearn' the country. This has meant challenging the status quo. Richard recalls hearing a beef industry leader at a Townsville conference in the late 1990s telling the audience that they did not need to spend much more on beef research because 'we know 95 per cent of what we need to know'. 'I thought this fellow was off the planet. Research is virtually non-existent in Northern Australia. We probably know only 5 per cent of what we need to know when moving from conventional management to holistic.'

To those who say kangaroos only should be farmed, Richard argues that the area's dry winter pastures are only digestible by cattle and white ants. 'Monogastric marsupials such as kangaroos follow our cattle onto short fresh grass and are increasing in numbers with the extra water and available feed. They could prove to be an additional valuable resource if we harvested them sustainably. Understand that to a large extent a cow doesn't live directly on grass. The bug populations in the rumen live on the grass breaking down and releasing energy and protein and the cow lives largely by digesting the bugs as they die off—a very different system from marsupials.'

Cattle have grazed the area around Julia Creek, the first European settlement in north-western Queensland, for around 140 years. Originally, the creek upon which the town is located

The loneliness of the road to Arizona. (Peter Rees)

was uninvitingly named Scorpion but, in 1870, it was changed to Julia Creek in honour of the niece of Donald Macintyre, who established the first property in the area.

Julia Creek's moment of importance came with the arrival of the railway in 1908, which meant the town became the railhead for north-western Queensland. The transport industry became the town's main economic justification until the railway moved on to Cloncurry and Mt Isa. The town achieved some small level of fame in Nevil Shute's book, *A Town Like Alice*, when the hero Joe Harman overlanded 1,400 cattle from the Gulf to Julia Creek. In the book, which later became a film, Joe stays at the fictional Post Office Hotel. This was obviously based on Gannon's Hotel, which is still over the road from the Post Office. Locals believe the fact that there is a Post Office Hotel in Cloncurry may mean that Shute was fictionally blending the two towns.

Like Cloncurry and so many of the towns in the Gulf region, Julia Creek with a population of 500 residents is now a service centre to a shire population of around 1,500 people, including the Makims. It is also the nearest thing to a neighbourhood community that the Makims have. They think little of making the two-hour drive from Arizona to Julia Creek for a rare chance to see a touring Brisbane theatre production, such as during the Centenary of Federation celebrations. A chance such as that to experience and enjoy culture and the arts is part of the social fabric that holds far-flung communities together.

Judi Makim understands this from long experience. 'I never really thought much of giving up the things that I liked to come here, which were concerts and live theatre and so forth,' she says. But she believes it is different with younger Australians. 'The next generation have those expectations that opportunities to experience the arts will be available. If you wanted to keep up that sort of lifestyle from here, you couldn't. Every so often we read about something that's on in the cities, and say that would be terrific, but you forget about it because it would cost a thousand dollars to get there and back, let alone accommodation. You pick and choose.'

Judi points to Townsville, at least nine hours away by car, or Mt Isa, four and a half hours away, as offsetting this to some extent—even though it is still a trip that means overnight accommodation, and travel time that would be beyond the range of most people. 'Townsville and Mt Isa are becoming centres for cultural amenities,' she says. 'The mentality where everything down south is still the best is changing, but it's people who are making it change. We have to start getting more infrastructure and development out here. Rural Australia produces $400 billion per annum for the nation, while less than one per cent is being returned. Perhaps this inequitable distribution is one of the reasons for some of the anger in the bush.'

For many people, the decision about whether to remain in towns like Julia Creek becomes less of an emotional and more of a practical one as services are closed down. In Julia Creek, the high school went back from Year 12 to Year 10. Banking services did not exist for a year after one of the 'Big Four'— the only one then in town—withdrew. At least now there is a building society, but loans are approved elsewhere. 'The GST has put a hell of a lot of onus back to the person doing the books,' Judi says. 'Unpaid office work has gone from two hours a day to five. Before, there was time for teaching. Now you've got to be an accountant as well.' For Judi, the importance of this can't be overemphasised, for she spent nineteen years home-schooling her children.

She recalls a recent visit from a travelling bush padre and his wife, who related that when they got to one station a day or so earlier the mother had just burst into tears, crying, 'Thank God you're here!' The padre and his wife visit homesteads where they stay a couple of days and help out if they're needed. 'His wife got into the kitchen, the mother into the office and he got into the classroom,' Judi says. 'The woman was trying to be the wife, mother, cook, garden and do the office—just too much.'

Disillusioned with the arguments for centralising head offices and operations further and further south, Richard Makim for the past decade has been in the vanguard of reasserting the power of local producers and communities. With the average age of graziers in the beef industry at about 60, he believes the writing is clearly on the wall unless they take hold of their future. 'To add insult to injury, we export our children and their futures here as well,' he says.

Towns like Julia Creek are suffocating under present unsustainable arrangements in the meat industry marked by low trust and low integrity. 'Growing a steer for two to three years and then stressing it out by taking it away from its social group and sticking it on a truck for a 1,000 to 2,000 km trip to the meatworks makes no sense,' Richard says. 'The producer has to bear the extra cost of sending the cattle further, and the end result is poor quality meat. It might be good for the bottom line of the big processing companies, but it's not for mine and it's terrible for the consumer's plate.'

For five years Richard sold his cattle to a major supermarket chain. 'I couldn't leave quickly enough. I got better and better at feeding them and they got worse and worse at feeding me. There was always a carrot dangled around the corner about how it was going to get better. It never did.'

One solution, Richard asserts, is to re-energise the concept of cooperatives or marketing groups. Individual private enterprise in a price-taker role has a limited future in globalisation, while shrinking competition constrains the proper functioning of market forces. As chairman of the North Australian Beef Co-operative (Beefco), he is seeking government and local community support to establish several independently owned and managed regional slaughter facilities to process up to 100 cattle a shift each, with a central boning and packing plant, probably in the Charters Towers or Townsville area. Associated products, such as hide and offal, would be returned to a tannery in Hughenden and a proposed pet snack plant in Julia Creek. Cattle would travel no more than 200 km to the abattoir. In all, he envisages processing around 500 head of cattle a day to make the plan work.

There are several hurdles to overcome, not least meat

inspection and producer and plant interdependence. But there would be jobs for five to ten slaughtermen at each abattoir, together with other jobs for storemen and packers and in administration. Local transport operators would benefit with daily live deliveries plus the same in cold shipping. The pet food factory would eventually employ about 30 people. Cattlemen would have the opportunity to retain ownership of their product through to cartons or beyond, with the overall operation ensuring community involvement.

After two decades of rationalisation of farms with the consequent impact on communities, he believes those who are still here 'are getting pretty adept at survival but also old and tired'. 'The last chances we can see are those of cooperative action. I don't see why large groups of private enterprise can't take bits of the capitalist and socialist systems and find a middle path. That's probably one of the answers to the future.'

Past mistakes in primary industry have taught painful lessons. Experience shows the failure of producers to own, integrate and manage all the steps necessary to succeed. Loss of control by the producer and the wider community by having processing done far away, and even overseas, has brought poor results for regional Australia. As one example Richard cites feral pigs, which contract shooters kill on properties such as his. The contract shooter gets about $1 a kilo delivered at Julia Creek. By the time the wild boar gets to a restaurant in Germany the price has soared to around $70 a kilo. 'I'd rather see the pigs go, but if they're going to be there, let's start making a business out of it and harvest them in a way that our communities benefit fairly.'

Richard is confident his plan will work. 'There's 20 per cent of people who are movers and shakers, innovators and entrepreneurs,' he says. 'Then there are the 60 per cent who are fence-sitters who watch and see what happens and probably knock it, but the minute it looks like happening they'll dive on it and say they thought of it. Then there's the other 20 per cent who will never change. That's across human nature. We've got to look for the entrepreneurs. I think the 60 per cent would come pretty fast if it worked. The thing about vision is that you have got to prepare for outright rejection initially. After three months, people begin to see the possibilities. In a further three months, having had time to mull it over, they get ownership of the idea.'

As Richard mused on his ideas and plans on the banks of the Saxby River, a sudden commotion erupted overhead. A wedgetail eagle had swooped on prey and in its talons now carried a squealing piglet back to its nest. 'Pigs can fly if you can provide enough lift and thrust,' Richard quipped. On Arizona, balance is at work.

Central
Parkes

BILL GIBBINS

For some people, there comes a time in their lives when there
is nothing else for it but a leap of faith. It is a time when circumstances propel a course of action that is inherently risky. Such
a time occurred for Bill Gibbins in the early 1970s when he
took stock of his job, his employers and the future direction of
the Australian transport industry. All of this added up to one
conclusion—take a chance, start your own transport company
and believe that you are right. Three decades later, with a
national transport business increasingly focused on the central
western New South Wales town of Parkes, there are many
people who are glad Bill Gibbins took that chance.

Aged 27, Bill had two young sons and with his wife, Iolanda,
had just bought their first house. Bill recalls telling her, 'If it all
goes bad we'll lose the house but it will probably take three
years to lose everything. We could finish up with nothing and

two kids by the time I'm thirty. But if that's the worst thing that can happen we'll be all right.' 'She went along with it,' Bill says. 'A bit of blind faith really. I borrowed $4,000. By the time I had spent $2,300 on such things as consignment notes and letter-head I had $1,700 left. That was my capital. I had to succeed right from the start or we were in big trouble.'

Bill was operations manager for a major transport company in Melbourne and knew that he had a secure career pathway ahead of him if he stayed. But various factors had come into play that caused him to question this. While the use of containers was still in its infancy, they had begun to revolutionise the movement of freight in Australia. However, shipping companies had a logistics problem: the containers that brought imported goods into Australia and were unloaded on the east coast needed to be transported to the port of Fremantle on the west coast where they had to be picked up for the return overseas journey.

The method for moving the containers from one side of the continent to the other was by old-fashioned coastal steamer. 'It was too slow and there were too many problems, such as strikes,' Bill says. 'I thought it should be on rail. So I left and started up the rail side of it.' FCL stands for Full Container Loads. The opportunity Bill saw was to load the empty boxes with domestic freight and rail them to Perth. The outcome was a potential win–win situation: he could offer big cost and time savings to clients wanting to get goods across the country, and he could also get the containers to Fremantle much more quickly for the shipping companies.

There was another factor that influenced Bill to establish his own company. When he was operations manager, one of his staff came to him asking for a pay rise. Bill went to management on

Tim Fischer inspects the FCL operations in Parkes. (Courtesy FCL)

his behalf but was told the worker was a troublemaker. Nonetheless, if he lifted his game they would reconsider a pay rise in three months' time. Three months later Bill went back to management and reported that the employee had increased his productivity. But the answer was the same as on the first occasion. When he went back a third time and management again refused a pay rise, Bill vowed he did not want to work for a company that gave false promises to staff. To this day, two-way trust is a fundamental principle of FCL.

In April 1974 Bill established FCL Interstate Transport Services. The beginnings were modest. He had one driver with a truck and a hired trailer, and just one client, a carpet manufacturer. And the economy was about to deteriorate. In June 1974, the first oil crisis hit when OPEC quadrupled the price of oil. 'People ask me now, how do you run a business in a recession? I say I started three months before one of the biggest recessions since the '30s. If you can handle that, you can handle anything. But you couldn't have picked a worse time to start,' Bill says.

Bill Gibbins is a nuggetty 'can-do' character with rugged, weather-beaten features and a sense of humour. He is just as at home in the corridors of power in Canberra as the freight yards around Melbourne. He's a hands-on managing director who still designs containers and trailers to suit the specific require-ments of customers. Parkes Mayor Robert Wilson has got to know Bill over the past few years. 'He calls a spade a spade. You get him upset, he swears, but that's normal for someone who had been in transport for over thirty years.' According to Mayor Wilson, Bill Gibbins is 'tough but terrific' to deal with.

Parkes is at the crossroads of the Newell Highway, connecting Melbourne and Brisbane, and the transcontinental railway link between Sydney and Perth. This means that two of the major transport corridors of Australia intersect at a town that for much of its life struggled for survival. Parkes began life as a hastily constructed tent town—first named Currajong, then Bush-mans—after gold was discovered in 1862. It was in 1873 that New South Wales Premier Sir Henry Parkes visited the local diggings. To honour the visit of the man who would later become the Father of Federation, the town was renamed after him. Twenty years later the railway line from Sydney reached Parkes, helping to transform the town from gold diggings to the centre of an increasingly prosperous agricultural district.

As the nineteenth century drew to a close, Henry Lawson, a revered son of the central west, noted the dramatic changes taking place in the bush with the rapid expansion of railways. To a boy who grew up on the nearby Gulgong goldfields, the steel tracks meant connection to the cities and beyond after the gold ran out as he portrayed it in his verse, *The Roaring Days*:

> The flaunting flag of progress
> In the West unfurled,
> The mighty bush with iron rails
> Is tethered to the world.

The idea of Parkes as a transport hub was first mooted in 1938, but it wasn't until 1969 that the Sydney–Perth standard gauge rail system was completed. Potentially, the completion meant that Parkes could be the marshalling and dispersal terminal for eastern Australia. The town could offer a viable single national distribution centre, not just for rail but also for road. Even the New South Wales Transport Minister of the day, Milton Morris, recognised this and tried to promote the idea. However, another three decades would pass before Bill Gibbins not only saw the potential, but acted on it—even after the frustration of a false start.

In 1984, Bill Gibbins wrote to the State Rail Authority of New South Wales seeking rates for freight operations out of Parkes. 'They gave us the average type of response, saying they were looking into it,' he remembers. 'But it must have been a bottomless pit they were looking into. No-one ever came back to me with prices.' All Bill got for his trouble was a speeding ticket on the way to Parkes. The idea went into limbo. Mayor Wilson recalls the council still had faith in rail and Goobang Junction and watched in frustration as the transport company leasing the site did nothing with it.

With the introduction of well-wagons in Australia in the mid-1990s, making it possible to stack two containers on top of each other, Bill began to again think seriously about Parkes.

In 1996, and with a major depot already established in Blayney near Bathurst, he made another visit to the town to inspect the Goobang Junction site, just 2 km outside Parkes. The junction was little changed from the flat, weed-infested rail head alongside the Sydney–Perth line that he'd seen twelve years earlier. When he returned to Melbourne he rummaged through old photographs and found some that he had taken of the site in 1984. The purple Paterson's curse weed of his earlier visit still blighted the area. However, this time there was more government interest. Bill bought 26 hectares and set about developing 2.5 ha as an intermodal rail and road terminal, reasoning that Goobang Junction was the closest point to the eastern seaboard for double-stacking containers on rail to Perth.

Mayor Wilson remembers it this way: 'We went out and chased Billy Gibbins down and harassed him until he came and made a commitment. But I'm not sure that Bill hadn't been angling for us to be aware of him. Anyway, he's put his money where his mouth is and he's expanding that investment. Billy is really the best disciple now of promoting the advantages of Parkes' geographical location from a logistics and transport perspective. We've certainly encouraged him and worked with him to assist him in achieving those goals.'

Goobang Junction has the potential to lock Parkes into the national economy in a way it never imagined. Opening the site with then Deputy Prime Minister Tim Fischer in May 1998, New South Wales Premier Bob Carr proclaimed Parkes as Australia's inland distribution centre. He noted that FCL had shown that Australians could offer something that was state-of-the-art in transport linkages. 'The tyranny of distance is a continuing theme in Australia's history, but this is the way to conquer it,' he said.

Bill Gibbins and his sons Andrew (middle) and Greg (right). (Courtesy FCL)

At the opening, one of the staff presented Bill Gibbins with a copy of a 1969 newspaper article in which the concept of Parkes as a national distribution centre was mooted. Bill's immediate thought was, 'What am I doing here? It's been around that long and it hasn't worked, how is it possibly going to work now?'

Each day, FCL tautliners—curtain-sided trailers—rumble along Australia's highways garbed with a side curtain displaying the image of Sir Henry Parkes that proclaims Parkes as the 'hub of the nation'. So far, FCL has outlayed $8 million developing Goobang Junction as a transport hub. Bill Gibbins has the capacity to strategically map out a vision and then get the job done. Headquartered in Melbourne where the Gibbins live, FCL today moves freight by rail, road and sea, but has specialist expertise in interstate linehaul by rail.

By 2001, the family-owned company was turning over more than $120 million a year. Each week FCL's Goobang Junction site handles more than 130 containers. Bill remains Chief Executive Officer, but increasingly sons Greg and Andrew are playing bigger leadership roles. 'The loyalty that people have for Bill is to walk across hot coals,' Greg, a Director, says. 'For my brother and me, that's the hardest thing that we have got to live up to. He has built the company on the philosophy of looking after his people, building and repaying trust. People work for Billy. The first two drivers who came with him still work for FCL. It's a family company, but a family within a family.'

That 'family' now includes a workforce of 45 in Parkes—as well as another 57 people in FCL depots in nearby Orange and Blayney and on a national basis, more than 500. The reason FCL is there is because of Bill's belief in the future of Parkes as the nation's distribution centre. Compared with the practice of operating warehouses in each capital city, the Parkes hub means overseas goods can be shipped into the port of Sydney, the containers transferred to Parkes by rail, stored in warehouses, and then distributed from there. Shipping containers are then assigned to exporters and railed full to any port in Australia. From a single warehouse in Parkes, products can be delivered overnight by rail and road to 82 per cent of Australia's population. And they can get to Perth more quickly and cheaply than any legal road operation. Perth may be 3,000 kilometres away, but by FCL's super freighter service out of Parkes it is just 48 hours. Bill reckons that makes Perth virtually a suburb of Parkes.

The hub city now hums. There is an almost palpable sense of optimism in the main street of Parkes, where major chain stores are now liberally represented. Allan Worrall, FCL's New South Wales Regional Manager, who lives 40 kilometres from

Parkes in Eugowra, says he has witnessed an 'emotional change' among people in the past three or four years since FCL opened. 'They now think there's a light at the end of the tunnel for their little town,' he says. 'The older people know now there is going to be a chance for their children to stay where they have grown up—not all of them obviously, but a chance for some of them because in any rural area the employment is probably negative rather than positive and some children need to move to the city. Now Parkes can see that the family unit may stay a little bit closer because of FCL and what it would bring to the area.'

But for many years the story could not have been more different. Pessimism infected the town. At the height of its operations in the 1950s, the New South Wales railways employed about 600 people in Parkes. Over the next three decades the number fell to as low as 40. People left to look for jobs elsewhere. One of those who left was Richard Guise who, as a twenty-year-old in 1985, went to Sydney to find work. It seemed to him that Parkes was going nowhere with little to keep young people entertained or employed. 'Besides sport, there wasn't a real lot to do around town,' he remembers. 'There was not even a picture theatre so we played sports six nights a week.' Richard spent the next fifteen years working in every capital city in Australia before returning as Parkes' fortunes changed. He sees a big change in the town in the years between his departure and return. 'We're too busy working now to be pessimistic,' he muses. 'It's the same lifestyle but the town has actually grown.' There are more amenities and more supermarkets. A cappuccino and reading the paper in an outdoor café may not be far off.

Citizens who achieve international sporting fame, such as

triple Olympic hockeyroo Stephen Davies, can expect street parades. Parkes likes to celebrate. On its annual agenda are a festival of sport at Easter, a jazz festival in June and a country music spectacular in October. There is even a weekend of celebration for Elvis Presley's birthday on 8 January each year. The Elvis Revival Festival was inaugurated in 1992 when Bob and Anne Steel thought something should be done to attract people to the town at a time of the year when most people wanted to leave the inland heat and head to the coast for holidays. There was nothing much to do in Parkes to keep people there, or indeed, to encourage people to visit.

Such is the power of Elvis that it was an immediate success at the aptly named Gracelands Convention Centre, a converted student hostel. 'I had 190 people at our restaurant for dinner on the first Friday night,' Anne Steel remembers. 'I thought that was pretty good, but I got quite a shock when a few thousand more people turned up on the Saturday.' Every January, Elvis impersonators flock to the town to perform, complete with white flairs and sideburns.

It has now become a celebration of the history of Australian rock music. Each year a plaque is unveiled on a wall to commemorate such rock icons as Johnny O'Keefe, Col Joye and Little Pattie. In 2001, as Australia celebrated Federation, the festival marked the occasion with t-shirts that had special significance to the town. People could be seen walking down the street with the face of Elvis on one side and that of Sir Henry Parkes on the other. This is a town that is now relaxed enough to have a sense of fun as well as history.

However, it was not Elvis Presley that brought Parkes into national—and indeed, international—focus but a movie based on the town's role in the first moon landing. Released in 2000,

The Dish was a box-office success with its story built around the 64-metre-wide, big-dish antenna radio telescope located 20 km outside the town. One of the most powerful telescopes in the world, the dish relayed signals for NASA's *Apollo 11* moonshot in 1969.

The film company, Working Dog Productions, hired the telescope for three weeks to make the movie, filming in Parkes and nearby Forbes. The film's release sparked interest in Parkes overseas. 'The reaction in England has been quite extraordinary,' Parkes development officer Michael Greenwood said soon after a visit to the UK. 'It has given us worldwide prominence. Tourism figures are up about 30 per cent since *The Dish*. We'd normally expect about 50,000 visitors a year at the telescope, but this year it will be more like 80,000. It's been a real hit for us.'

As Sydney prepared for the 2000 Olympics, Parkes added its own touch. On its journey to Homebush Bay, the Olympic torch passed through Parkes. Images of Mayor Wilson carrying the flame were beamed around the world on the same telescope that had conveyed images of Neil Armstrong's 1969 moonwalk. That walk made Parkes the centre of the universe for a fleeting moment, memories of which *The Dish* and Robert Wilson's own run rekindled. However, the task Parkes now faces is more mundane but no less important—to become the centre for freight distribution in Australia.

FCL's commitment to the development of the Goobang Junction site as a national hub may have more to do with geography and the accidental development of the nation's transport routes, but for Parkes it has far-reaching consequences. For a town that has often struggled against adversity, the development represents a chance to secure a major economic toehold. People are now witnessing growth that seemed just a dream as the town stagnated in the mid-1980s.

For most of its history after the railway reached the town, government infrastructure was the focus of employment for Parkes, as indeed it was for many country towns. Even in the early 1980s one in three jobs in Parkes was in local, state, or federal government. Now with the growth in the private sector it is more like one in five. The town has broken free of the government hand-out mentality. 'It's different in Parkes,' Allan Worrall says. 'It's more an attitude of "let's get on with it and don't worry about what they're doing in Sydney". That attitude seems to have done us a hell of a lot better than having a whinge.'

A lifeline for the town came with the opening of a mine in the early 1990s to extract copper and gold from two open cut and one underground mine. The Northparkes mine, which is the biggest employer in the area, with about 300 workers, provided a solid base for the rebuilding process, bringing people back to the town and encouraging construction of new homes.

A mini housing boom followed, with the construction of 500 new homes in four years. A disused second gold mine 2 km outside the town has also re-opened, crushing the old over-burden to make road-base. A third mine that will extract nickel and cobalt is proposed in Lachlan Shire, 60 km away. With an estimated life of more than 40 years, it will be bigger than Northparkes, require 1,000 workers in the construction phase and 300 once it opens. Another potential component of the rebuilding process is the plan by the Inland Marketing Corporation to build an international freight airport at Parkes to link New South Wales agricultural producers with world markets, especially in the Asia–Pacific region.

Michael Greenwood says that with FCL, Austop and the mining, Parkes is 'able to hold a fair percentage of kids here when that is so often not the case in other towns'. Because Parkes no longer depends entirely on returns from the surrounding farming community, residents have begun to look at the town differently. Before, the outlook was predominantly agricultural. If the cockies had a good year then the town was going ahead, but if the farmers had a bad year there were long faces.

Now, that's not so much the case. Farming is still a key part of the community, but no longer the whole community. Other industries are now underpinning the economy and creating jobs, not least in transport and mining.

Greg Gibbins has no doubt that the key to Parkes' success as a distribution hub is information technology. 'You can now have a distribution facility physically in the middle of nowhere and still be able to communicate with the rest of the world,' he says. 'In the past there were no IT [information technology] systems capable of delivering this live data. The idea of hubs has been around a long time, but it's the IT advancements that actually make it viable these days.' FCL closely monitors container progress through sophisticated computer tracking systems, and is continually adapting new technology such as data loggers, barcodes and scanners.

Greg Gibbins says that compared with traditional labouring and farming jobs, which will always be at risk in the bush due to the whim of world markets, the advent of transport hubbing is bringing new employment opportunities, such as IT systems programmers. As companies relocate to transport hubs, jobs such as warehouse managers, forklift operators and drivers are also created. All these jobs are transferable to other cities and towns. 'It is not a BHP in Newcastle, it's not a steel mill that will shut down leaving people with no long term employment,' he says. 'The skills required in transport and logistics are transferable to any city in the country.'

Parkes Shire Council general manager, Alan McCormack, says some big companies are starting to evaluate the cost benefits of setting up in the town, and the catalyst for this is principally FCL. 'FCL started it all and there is potential for them to have a very major impact on Parkes,' he says. 'FCL is certainly the cornerstone of major development, I would think, especially with the Port Augusta-Alice Springs-Darwin line when it becomes operational around 2004. We think that will have great potential for Parkes as it will link up with the east–west line.' The council is also hopeful that the proposed Melbourne to Brisbane and Darwin rail project, which would pass through Parkes, will go ahead. The scheme's proponents say that with it, Parkes will become another Chicago and, they suggest, double its population.

Companies that have been attracted by the cost savings offered by the Parkes hub include Elders, which owns a wool top making and combing plant alongside Goobang Junction, Bridgestone Tyres, which does all of its rural distribution out of Parkes, Australia Post and Australian Paper Manufacturers. The rail haulage operator, Silverton Tramways, has moved its operations from Broken Hill to Parkes in a further sign of confidence in the town's economic future. A Canadian company, Bourgault, which assembles agricultural equipment, is another company to base its Australian operations there. Greg Gibbins says he is often asked how FCL will get people to live in Parkes. 'My response is, it's a safe town, people don't worry about their kids walking home from school or from friends at night,' he says. 'That's something unheard of in our capital cities these days.'

Despite the bright prospects for Parkes, the Gibbins are cautious about the future. Greg Gibbins says that with the bursting of the IT bubble in the past couple of years, companies want to see the system working before they will move operations to Parkes. 'It's not a case of us going out, telling everybody and flooding the market and having people bombard us wanting to go to Parkes,' he says. 'It's a case of getting it up, having it work. We're crawling before we walk, walking before we run. Our goal is to get an ironclad conduit of a distribution facility at Parkes that will work on a small scale. The greatest success will come when a company boss gets up at an annual conference and announces big cost savings as a result of warehousing in Parkes. Once it's proven that the conduit is operational and efficient you will be able to put as much as you want through there. But you only get one shot at it.'

Parkes, it could be said, is on target.

Railroaded

QUORN

If Parkes is the nation's modern railway hub, then the South Australian town of Quorn could have laid claim to this title for most of the first half of the twentieth century. Located near the Flinders Ranges, 345 kilometres north of Adelaide, the years between World War I and II were Quorn's boom period. It flourished as a grand railway junction, playing host to a long list of prominent people.

Among the visitors was Edward, Prince of Wales, who travelled to Quorn in July 1920 while on a royal visit to Australia. Edward, who went on to briefly become Edward VIII before abdicating, was accompanied by Earl Mountbatten and a large royal entourage. Huge crowds turned out at Quorn to welcome them all and the mayor of the day took the prince on a short walk up the main street.

Clearly, the prince was kept very busy in Quorn and was unable to escape the public eye. In contrast, when he reached Sydney he sought to relax on a cruise on Sydney Harbour. This cruise was to become notorious, for it spawned rumours—true or false—that he went below decks with a lady friend. Nine months after this antipodean interlude she is said to have given birth to a baby boy.

Quorn at the time of the future Edward VIII's visit was near its zenith. Prime ministers (most notably John Curtin), diplomats, bureaucrats, business people, farmers and, above all else, members of the armed forces travelled through Quorn by train. During World War II, Quorn was a vital railway junction. Military, coal and other traffic placed heavy demands on the railway with more than a million troops travelling through the town. Even General Douglas MacArthur travelled to Quorn by troop train in March 1942. Stuart Holland and Ollie McHugh, who made the return run between Alice Springs and Quorn each week from 1939 to 1945, remember the trip well. The future Supreme Commander of the South West Pacific Area boarded the train with his family in Alice Springs and Stuart and Ollie, who are both now in their eighties, steamed south at a snail's pace on the narrow gauge 3ft 6in (106,7cm) railway. The trip took three days and they saw little of the general, who kept to himself. What they remember most is the food the American troops offered them. 'That Yankee tinned stuff was out of this world,' Stuart Holland told the *Australian* in March 2002 on the sixtieth anniversary of the trip.

On the morning of 20 March, the train pulled into Quorn, where the ladies of the Country Women's Association had prepared a breakfast of rissoles and mash. By mid-afternnon the train reached the dust bowl of Terowie, where the narrow gauge ended and the broad gauge began. MacArthur transferred to a pair of luxury carriages provided by the South Australian Railways commissioner. Today, a plaque on the platform serves as a reminder that before he left MacArthur once again uttered his famous fighting words, 'I shall return'.

Quorn was named after Quorndon in the English county of Leicestershire, and the area was developed by pastoralists who moved north from Adelaide in the mid-nineteenth century. In 1878, just down the track at Port Augusta, then South Australian Governor Sir William Jervois turned the sod for the first railway to Quorn, saying at the time, 'This will help connect Australia and its trade to such places as India, Siam and China.' Sadly this particularly narrow gauge line, which was envisaged to go through to Katherine and Darwin, never made it beyond Alice Springs.

However, it did make it to Quorn, ultimately leading to the connection back to Adelaide via Peterborough and Terowie and northward to the town that would subsequently be named Marree. Quorn became a national crossroad for Sydney–Perth rail traffic and the Adelaide–Alice Springs railway, particularly through the 1920s and 1930s.

In the early 1920s a passenger train ran from Terowie through Quorn before terminating at Oodnadatta. A sleeping carriage was part of the train, and on one occasion an Afghan passenger alighted at Quorn to recite his evening prayers. Railwaymen dubbed the train the *Afghan Express*. This soon became folklore, and in time was abbreviated to *The Ghan*. The service, with its distinctive timber-bodied carriages, was extended to Alice Springs in 1926.

Two million concrete sleepers and 1,420 kilometres of track are now being laid from Alice Springs to the port of Darwin so that by 2004 the modern standard gauge *Ghan* will finally make it into Darwin. In one sense, this will be 80 years late, as Federal governments have promised South Australia such a rail connection for virtually every decade since the 1920s, failing of course to deliver. As recently as 1983 the first steps in building the line had been made north of the Alice Springs railyards. But in March that year the government changed and Bob Hawke replaced Malcolm Fraser as prime minister. Shortly after, he shelved the whole project. Perhaps the spirit of John Flynn of the Inland influenced John Howard and John Anderson when they decided to complete the project.

Indeed, fate has dealt Quorn a loaded hand. For more than a century the town has been frustrated by being in the right location in one sense but in the wrong location in another. And as the world's largest transcontinental railway project now unfolds between Adelaide, Alice Springs and Darwin, Quorn once again battles the problem of being so near yet so far.

The town already knows that what a railway may confer, it can just as easily take away. In 1937 a direct route was opened to the west using standard gauge from Port Pirie to Port Augusta and connecting to the existing Port Augusta Commonwealth Rail to Kalgoorlie. In the 1960s, standard gauge was extended into Perth, and when the connection was completed between Port Augusta and Broken Hill, and finally from Crystalbrook to Adelaide, it meant Quorn had been completely bypassed. All by less than 50 kilometres.

After the war, other than occasional local freight services, rail went into steep decline in the area until the Pichi Richi Railway Preservation Society was formed. In 1974 operations started again out of Quorn Railway Station, steam trains initially travelling only short distances, but these days running into Port Augusta. The extension of the line into Port Augusta has opened up another gateway into the Flinders Ranges.

Now in the twenty-first century a hive of activity has returned to Quorn through dint of hard work and local leadership. Quorn these days has a population of around 1,400 people and has become a small rural service town and council headquarters. Steadily growing tourism flowing from the efforts of the Pichi Richi Railway Preservation Society and an active local council now underpin the revival of Quorn's rich railway heritage.

The main focus has been the work of members of the Preservation Society. Teams of volunteers have patiently restored the railway link from the town to Woolshed Flat and then through the Pichi Richi Pass on the edge of the Flinders Ranges to Stirling North, where it meets today's standard gauge east–west and north–south railway mainline.

As the great north–south transcontinental railway project to Darwin unfolds, the Pichi Richi Railway will be ready to connect with it. When it does, it will be a reminder of the role of the railways in Australia's history—and not least the role that the transcontinental railway played a century ago when it was an important factor in convincing Western Australia to become part of the Australian Federation.

The transcontinental railway project will also be a victory for the local communities and their mayors, particularly Mayor Joy Baluch of Port Augusta. She is a colourful character who has been mayor for many years and has been singleminded about developing rail for the twenty-first century. Ask Joy about opposition to rail expansion, and she replies, 'Anyone standing in the way of the railway can f*** off, I hope you understand this. God bless'. While this is not necessarily the language used by other community leaders in the Iron Triangle, they are all nonetheless as one in supporting the resurgence of rail and the Darwin project.

Late in 2001 Robert Gerard, head of the electrical company Clipsal and board member of the Australian Chamber of Commerce and Industry, travelled on the Pichi Richi train at dusk en route to the Willows Restaurant just outside Quorn. He was struck by the potential for evening trains to have searchlights and floodlights mounted on the roof of the passenger carriages to highlight the steep slopes and colourful rock faces of the spectacular and narrow Pichi Richi Pass by night. It appears that, finally, the lights are on in Quorn.

Reaching for
the Stars

There is a positive way ahead for rural and regional Australia, one that will attract new investment and new people. Driven by local communities and local people, it builds on the foundations of what has been achieved in the bush over generations. But in the process the unwritten pact between the cities and the Outback, on which Australia was built, will need to be reassessed and given new meaning.

Fundamental to the pact was the understanding that regional and rural Australia would not be left behind, that health, education, roads and communications were a right for all Australians, regardless of whether they lived in the city or the bush. While bush communities have succeeded more often than not in spite of government policies, from the days of European settlement governments have provided an important framework through land grants, tax breaks and cheap loans to development projects such as the Snowy Mountains Scheme. These were times when the mood of the nation could be captured by Banjo Paterson's potent imagery of 'the vision splendid of the sunlit plains extended'. Whether you lived in Toorak or Tibooburra the sentiment resonated.

The vision is no longer quite so splendid. In the past twenty years or so, social and economic changes have undermined the egalitarianism on which the city–country pact was built. There is ample evidence to suggest that the position of rural and regional Australia is worsening when compared with metro-politan Australia, and indeed, that the position of smaller towns is worsening in relation to larger regional centres. The loss of banking and telecommunications services and government agencies have left country people stressed and their communities debilitated. The consequence overall has been declining social cohesion with increased suicide and mental health problems in rural areas and a lack of trust in government.

The plight of small towns is perhaps exemplified by events in Merriwa in July 1999. Protesting against the impending removal of a demountable classroom, people formed a human chain around the town's school. Their aim was to prevent the loss of what they regarded as a piece of essential community infrastructure. One of the protesters told the media that the attempt to remove the demountable was '. . . an insult to the whole of regional New South Wales'.

That is one end of the spectrum. At the other, for many Indigenous Australians living in small towns the desperation is even more personal. With inadequate health standards their life expectancy is twenty years less than other Australians, and income levels and employment rates are unacceptably low. All too often they feel outsiders in their own land.

One way or another, there are many factors that contribute to the depressing mood. The ten years after 1991, for example, saw a loss of 66,000 regional railway jobs. In the five years from the mid–1990s more than 10,000 rural bank jobs disappeared, almost solely due to loss of bank branches and staff positions because of electronic banking. Asa Wahlquist has estimated that in the decade to 1996, up to 30,000 jobs in service industries disappeared from regional New South Wales alone.

Too often the protests of the bush have been dismissed as a mantra of doom and gloom. Not surprisingly, the result has been a general feeling among people outside the capital cities that they have been ignored. It should therefore come as no surprise that there is a growing tide of determination to confront the view that rural and regional Australia is heading nowhere with no new investment, no new jobs, no profits and no progress.

Politically, the result has been the election of more Independents to the federal and state parliaments in protest against government policies. In the 10 November 2001 federal election, for instance, two additional Independents were elected, taking the number in the House of Representatives to three—all of them from rural and regional Australia. Support for Independents, however, does fluctuate. The New South Wales by-election for the regional seat of Tamworth at the end of 2001 saw this key seat, previously held by a high-profile Independent for more than a decade, revert to the National Party.

The reality is, of course, that the days of the high tariff wall against overseas imports are gone. Australia is a trading nation, and to compete it has to remain leaner than its competitors. It already is the most efficient farming nation in the world, but mechanisation and competition for markets mean that this demand will continue. The problem is that this places pressure not just on family farms but also the country towns that service them. The political challenge for governments is to manage and minimise the inevitable pain of change—something that has not

The HMAS *Otway* in the main street of Holbrook. (Courtesy of Holbrook Shire Council)

always been achieved. The sheer expanse of Australia, not to mention the harshness of the landscape, has made this particularly difficult.

Australia is a continent where the lack of navigable inland rivers, plus the barrier of the Great Dividing Range, have acted as counters to the nation's growth and determined where population centres are located. With the exception of Queensland where Rockhampton, Mackay, Townsville and Cairns counterbalance Brisbane, Australia is more centralised than most large nations. Despite its flawed history, decentralisation thus remains a goal if the drift to the cities through the attraction of higher incomes and better jobs is to be counteracted, for the loss of young people deprives communities of not just a socially active group but also potential leaders.

The role of leadership is central, for community action can make a substantial difference to economic outcomes at the local level. As New South Wales regional development policy expert Paul Collits puts it, regional leaders, whether through regional boards, local government, development bodies or 'main street' committees, can energise their communities in the pursuit of strategic investment opportunities. 'Leaders can mobilise a range of resources and enthuse their regions. Leaders can leverage opportunities provided through a wide source of funding mechanisms. Leaders can create vision at the local level and formulate strategies for survival.'[1]

With this in mind, the role of government in regional development these days is essentially one to facilitate progress in bush communities. Governments can act as a catalyst, with local communities themselves driving change. Behind this philosophy is a realisation that governments on their own do not have the resources to deliver regional prosperity. Rather, it will come from community 'ownership' of problems and solutions. As such, governments and development agencies have begun to recognise the importance of communities rebuilding from the 'bottom up' and 'inside out'. No longer is it 'top down' and 'outside in'. Consequently, a range of technical assistance and funding schemes to foster rural renewal has emerged.

At the same time, governments must also continue to provide essential infrastructure for regional communities and deliver services that are accessible and maintain the regional quality of life if the city–country pact is to continue to have meaning.

---

1   Paul Collits, Manager Policy, NSW Department of State and Regional Development, paper presented to the Future of Australia's Country Towns Conference at La Trobe University, Bendigo, June 2000.

On one level this means that after decades of line closures, rail is undergoing a revival that will bring tangible benefits to Outback producers and communities. Most notably, construction of the Alice Springs to Darwin standard gauge rail link is in full swing. This will complete a crucial link to the port located closest to Asia on the Australian mainland. Markets in Asia will be brought closer and it will cost less to get there. Contributing also to the rail revival is a change in culture whereby for the first time internal rail competition is replacing inefficient state government railway monopolies.

Although Australia still has five operating railway gauges, all mainland capital cities nonetheless are connected by standard gauge. Already, rail carries 80 per cent of Australia's east–west freight across the Nullarbor, and the inland rail proposal through Victoria, New South Wales and Queensland will consolidate the new role of rail in the bush. The bulk of Australia's population will continue to hug the coastline population centres, but such a project must encourage decentralisation and augurs well for Outback communities.

Initiatives like this, however, are not the complete story. The key is people and communities like those in this book. They are examples of what can be done in the Outback through vision, determination and a willingness to have a go. They represent individual and local success stories—some of them big, some of them modest. They are successful because they learn from mistakes and are determined to see their goal through. They are successful because in adversity they see opportunity. They are representative of a never-say-die spirit that has served Australia well for two centuries.

As their stories show, there is plenty of initiative in the bush. Some communities may be stuck in a time warp and, indeed,

The historic steam train journey from Quorn to Port Augusta follows the route of the Afghan Express. (Courtesy of the Pichi Richi Railway Preservation Society)

not all of them can or will survive. But for every town or village in decline there will always be another where, through local dynamics, leadership and energy, people and businesses are succeeding.

It is through the grit of individuals such as Roger Fletcher and Tom O'Toole that the bush will advance. Starting with nothing, they overcame obstacles and doubters to achieve their goals and, in the process, provide jobs. Then there is the inspiration of Peter and Judy Howarth and Richard and Judi Makim who, hundreds of kilometres apart, are applying the principles of holistic management to their farms and communities.

Add in the foresight of Bill Gibbins with his Parkes rail hub, Steve and Karen Birkbecks' ingenuity and application in taking their product from kitchen stove to international markets, the innovativeness of Mick Denigan in using a car battery to fire up his web page on the internet, the leadership and drive of Jane Bennett, and the bush is in good hands.

These are the people who have seen past the Outback bars to the stars. They are the way forward but they are not alone. There are many more heroes out there, Outback—just as there are many more communities that truly count.

Acknowledgements

This book evolved through discussions with our publisher, John Iremonger, who shared our belief that the story of people and communities outside urban limits in contemporary Australia was a much more positive and exciting one than commonly thought. We offer our gratitude to John.

As this book has unfolded there are other people we would like to thank. Among them are Jodie O'Sullivan, Pat Gill and Rob Linn for help with photos and background material; Sue Langford for her insightful advice; and Rebecca Kaiser, our editor, advisor and soundingboard for coordinating the project from beginning to end.

We would also like to thank our families for their support throughout this long project, and finally, our thanks to all the people in this book for their openness and support for the concept.

Index

radio stations 91, *92*, 94-6, 100
railways 197-201, 203, 206-7; *see also* transport industry
Ralston Purina company (USA) 23
RAN Submarine Squadron 107-8
raspberries processing 54
Redpath, Jean 69
restaurant, *see* Salopian Inn
Rockleigh property, Quirindi 149
Rotary Club 60, 61
Royal Australian Navy submarines 107-9
Rural Transaction Centre Advisory Panel 53

Salopian Inn, McLaren Vale 134-8
sandalwood oil industry 4, 73-7, 83-9
Santalia (sandalwood) label 73, 77
Savory, Allan 149-52, 171
Sawtrey, Hugh 97
School of Distance Education, Longreach 100
Schubert, Max 131
Seaview winery 128
Serisier, Jean 12
Shalaks, company 82, 83
Sharp, Sandra 129
Shear Outback project, Hay 9-10
sheepmeat industry 4, 11-23
Shute, Nevil 176
Sirocco (band) 69-70
Smith, Allan 12, 18, 20
Sorell, Governor 54
Steel, Anne 191
Steel, Bob 191
Stockman's Hall of Fame, Longreach 9, 90, 97-8
Stoker, Lt H. 107
Strang, Alan 100

Strang, Robin 90, 100, 101-2
submarines 106-9

Tamworth Country Music Festival 120
Tasmanian Cottage Industry Exhibition and Craft Fair 61
Tasmanian Rural Industry Training Board 53, 59
Tasmanian Tidy Towns award 61
Terry, Ned 62
Thomson, Sir Edward Deas 93
Thomson River 93, 99
Throssell, Jim 6
timber industry 155
Tjulyuru Cultural and Civic Centre, Warburton 7, 160, 162-4
Tocumwal 30, 43
Toole, Christopher 30
Toole, Nona 30
tourism 28, 70, 97, 99, 106, 137, 138, 146-7, 155-6, 158, 192
Tower Hill, Port Fairy 67
Tracy Memorial Award, RAIA 162
transport industry 182-90, 192, 195; *see also* railways
Trott, Greg 130, 132, 133, 138-9
Trott, Roger 130
truffles 54
Two Mad Hatters 90, 100-2

Uluru 159, 165
United Milk Tasmania, Wynyard 55

Victorian Tourism Awards 41, 70
Viegas, Albie 161, 163
vineyards 125-34, 139-41
Visyboard company 26

Wagga Wagga 5
Wahgunyah 27